KU-496-993

The Concise Encyclopedia of

The Concise Encyclopedia of

BIRDS

by Bertel Bruun
Illustrated by Paul Singer

SOUTH DEVON TECHNICAL
COLLEGE LIBRARY

Octopus Books

This book
is dedicated to
two of my oldest friends
and teachers in ornithology,
Johannes Ferdinand
and Ole Schelde.

This edition first published 1974 by
Octopus Books Limited
59 Grosvenor Street, London W1

Produced by Vineyard Books, Inc., New York

© Vineyard Books, Inc., New York

ISBN 0 7064 0365 7

Printed in Italy by A. Mondadori, Verona

Introduction

This book is intended as a precise and easy-to-use reference work for birdwatchers and bird lovers—novices and experts alike. The entries are arranged alphabetically, and because of the extensive cross-referencing, no index has been deemed necessary.

The entries include all the orders and all the families of living birds. In general, single species are not included. As the orders of birds are to be found under their scientific names, a list giving both the scientific and the common names is found in an appendix on page 239. The families are listed under their common names only. In some cases, particularly of large families, entries describe the sub-groups into which these families are divided. This encyclopedia also includes entries on the anatomy, physiology and behavior of birds. Furthermore, short biographical notes about more prominent ornithologists of the past, as well as some of the individuals after whom birds have been named, are given. Special terms used in ornithology are defined but no attempt has been made to include those which are in general use. Terms printed in *italics* (except such items as book titles) indicate related articles to which the reader is referred. For example, in the article on migration there are cross-references to *banding, irruption* and *orientation*. A highly selected bibliography appears on page 237.

BERTEL BRUUN

Black-footed albatross

A

ABDOMEN: the part of the body between the chest and pelvis containing most of the *alimentary canal*, the kidneys, and the organs of the *reproductive system*. Also called belly.

ABERT, JAMES WILLIAM (1820–1897): American officer who collected birds. Abert's towhee is named after him.

ABMIGRATION: abnormal *migration*.

ABRASION: wear of *feathers*.

ACCENTOR: a member of Prunellidae, an Old World family of sparrow-sized, soft-billed, drab-colored birds. The twelve species inhabit brushlands where they find their insect food.

Alpine accentor

ACCIPITER: a member of the subfamily Accipitrinae, in North America represented by the species of goshawk, Cooper's hawk, and sharp-shinned hawk. All are forest-dwelling *birds of prey* with rounded wings and long tails. They live on other birds caught in the air.

Goshawk

ADAPTION: the development of change that makes an organism, organ, or reaction more fit for a given environmental pressure.

ADULT: an animal that has reached sexual maturity, including secondary sexual characters, *plumage* in particular.

AERIE: the nest of a *bird of prey*, particularly that of an *eagle*.

AFTERSHAFT: a small *feather* of the same origin, but underlying the regular feather.

Feather with large aftershaft

AGGRESSION: the behavior of antagonism, especially referring to intraspecific behavior. Aggression in the form of overt attack is rare among birds, but more subtle expression in the form of threatening posturing is common, especially when a *territory* is being defended. *Display* of brightly colored plumage parts is often part of aggressive behavior.

AIGRETTE: a special *feather* grown by egrets in their *nuptial* plumage. Due to their softness and beauty, these feathers were widely used by the millinery industry, which almost caused the extermination of egrets in North America. Protection, especially sponsored by the Audubon Society, together with changes in fashion, saved these members of the *heron* family.

AIR SAC: a thin-walled expansion of the *respiratory system* of birds,

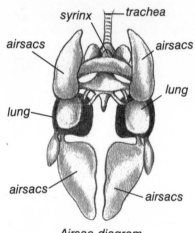

Airsac diagram

involving the thoracic, abdominal, as well as other cavities. Air sacs are closely connected with the lungs and aid in breathing as well as in making the bird lighter.

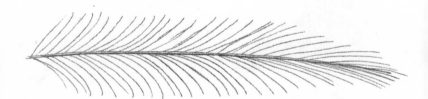

Aigrette

Wandering albatross

ALBATROSS: a member of the family Diomedeidae. Albatrosses are long-winged (11½ feet in the wandering albatross), somewhat gill-like birds of the open seas. They are clumsy on land, but swim well and are expert flyers. Their colors are white, black, and brown. The thirteen species are mostly found in the Southern Hemisphere. Their food consists of plankton, fish, and other aquatic animals. They nest in large colonies, mainly on islands. The black-footed albatross can be seen off the West Coast of North America.

ALBINO: a bird with abnormal plumage in which all pigment is absent, including the *soft parts* and the iris. The birds are white with the eyes appearing red. Partial albinos with only certain areas of the plumage being white occur.

ALBUMEN: the egg white that surrounds the *yolk*, but is enclosed within the membranes and the shell of the *egg*.

ALIMENTARY CANAL: also called the digestive tract. The alimentary canal stretches from the bill to the anus. As food passes through the alimentary canal it is broken down by mechanical and chemical means and nutrients and water are absorbed. The waste material is expelled through the anus as *droppings*.

In a bird the alimentary canal begins with the mouth and its *bill*. As birds lack teeth, no chewing is done and the food is swallowed in lumps. The esophagus leads from the mouth to the stomach. Off the lower part of the esophagus is a saclike outpouching known as the crop. The crop differs in size

9

from species to species and is largest in grain-eating birds like pigeons and fowl. Food can be stored here and then regurgitated to feed young. In pigeons the crop secretes a protein-rich fluid called pigeon's milk.

The avian stomach consists of two parts: the proventriculus is rather thin-walled and mainly serves as a secreting organ where the enzymes and acid necessary for the breakdown of food are produced. The second part of the avian stomach is the gizzard, which has strong muscular walls that break up the food particles with grinding movements. In grain-eating birds the gizzard muscle is extremely strong. Grain-eaters will often swallow stones and pebbles (grit), which collect in the gizzard and aid in the breakup of food. From the stomach the food passes into the small intestine, where enzymes from the pancreas and bile from the liver are added. During its passage through the small intestine, the food continues to be digested and the nutrients are absorbed. From the small intestine the food enters the large intestine, which at its beginning is supplied with two long, blind tubes where nutrients as well as water are absorbed. From the large intestine the waste product enters the *cloaca*, where urine also collects. The mixture is finally deposited as *droppings*.

ALLEN, CHARLES ANDREW (1841–1930): American carpenter and amateur ornithologist. Allen's hummingbird is named after him.

ALLOPATRIC: a term used to designate species or families living in different geographic areas.

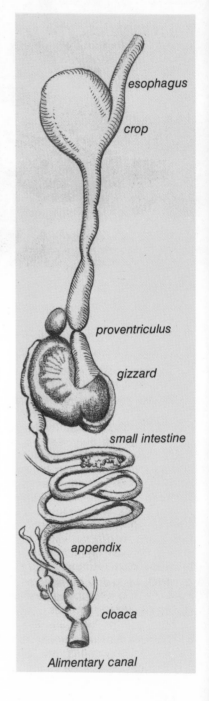

Alimentary canal

esophagus

crop

proventriculus

gizzard

small intestine

appendix

cloaca

Anhinga

ALTRICIAL: a term denoting a young bird incapable of locomotion when hatched.

ALULA: see *bastard wing*.

ANHINGA: also called a snakebird or darter. Anhingas are closely related to the *cormorants*. They are water birds with very long, thin necks and pointed bills. The plumage is mainly black or dark brown. The two species of anhingas live in inland swamps and lakes in the warmer parts of the Americas, Africa, Asia, and Australia where they catch fish under water, frequently by spearing them on their bills. They often swim partially submerged so that only the head and neck are visible. Anhingas nest in colonies in bushes or trees.

ANI: one of the three species of black long-tailed birds related to the *cuckoos*. Anis are found in the subtropical and tropical parts of the New World. They are gregarious in habits and build communal nests in which several females may deposit their eggs. Both smooth-billed anis and groove-billed anis occur in the southernmost parts of the United States.

Smooth-billed ani

ANSERIFORMES: an order comprising the *screamers*, *ducks*, *geese*, and *swans*.

ANTBIRD: a member of the family Formicariidae. Antbirds are small, rather dull-colored, soft-billed birds inhabiting tropical and mountain forests of Central and South America. The family consists of about 230 species. The predilection for ants found in a few of the species has given the family its name. Species like ant thrushes, antshrikes, antwrens, and antvireos belong to this family.

White-faced antcatcher

ANTHROPOMORPHISM: the description or interpretation of animal behavior in terms of human behavior and emotion. Such descriptions and interpretations are no longer considered valid and should be avoided.

ANTING: behavior in which ants are applied to the feathers by the bird itself. In this way chemicals excreted from the ants, particularly formic acid, are smeared on the feathers where they may have a cleansing action. Only certain species are prone to anting; among these are the starlings and blue jays.

ANTIPHONAL SONG: a special kind of singing performed by certain, mainly tropical species in which the two members of a pair alternate in singing different phrases of the song with such accurate timing that it is virtually impossible to tell that the song is being performed by two birds rather than one.

APODIFORMES: an order comprising the *swifts* and *crested swifts*.

APTERYGIFORMES: an order containing the family of *kiwis*.

ARCHAEOPTERYX: a *fossil bird* from the Jurassic period (135 to 180 million years ago). The archaeopteryx differed from modern birds mainly by having teeth. Its feathers, however, classified it as a bird, and made it capable of gliding, although probably not active flight. The archaeopteryx forms a link with the

Archaeopteryx fossil

J.F. Audubon's "The Birds of North America" included 435 individual plates. This monumental work is unsurpassed in the ornithological literature in respect to artistic beauty.

reptilian ancestors of birds. Three specimens are known, all found in Germany. One is exhibited in London, the other two in Germany.

ARDEIFORMES: an order containing the families of *ibises* and *spoonbills*, *herons* and *bitterns*, *hammerheads*, *shoebill storks*, and *storks*.

ASITY: a member of the family Philepittidae. The four species of asities are limited in distribution to the forests of Madagascar. They are small, mainly black and yellow, solitary birds.

AUDUBON, JOHN JAMES (1785–1851): American ornithologist, born in Hispaniola. After spending a short time in France as a boy, he moved to the United States where he studied painting and at first made a living as a portrait painter. However, he became interested in ornithology and through his creation of the double elephant-folio work *The Birds of America* became the most famous nature painter in the world. *The Birds of America* was completed in 1838. Besides being a superb artist, Audubon was a most active ornithologist who added much to our knowledge of birds. He was honored by having three birds named after him, Audubon's caracara, Audubon's warbler and Audubon's shearwater.

AUK: a member of the family Alcidae. Auks are medium-sized diving birds that spend most of their time at sea. Their plumage is generally black and white. The wings are short. Auks live mainly on fish caught under water. One species, the greak auk, has become extinct in historic times. It was distributed along the coasts of the northern part of the North Atlantic. The last great auk was killed in Iceland in 1848. Its inability to fly made it an easy prey for hungry fishermen. The twenty-one living species of auks are distributed over the North Atlantic and Northern Pacific. Auklet, guillemot, murre, murrelet, and puffin are names for members of this family. Most auks nest in colonies along seashores, either on inaccessible cliff ledges or in holes among boulders or dug into the turf.

AVES: the scientific name for the class of *birds*.

AVICULTURE: the practice of keeping wild birds in capitivity for the purpose of studying and breeding them. Aviculture has become important in the attempt to save threatened species. The most successful example is that of the Hawaiian goose. Threatened by extinction in its native habitat, some captive specimens of this beautiful goose were successfully bred in captivity by the Wild Fowl Trust in England in the early 1950's and a large flock established in captivity. From this stock the species could be reintroduced into the wild. Attempts are also being made to build up a captive stock of the threatened whooping crane.

AVIFAUNA: the birdlife of a limited geographic area.

Razorbill

European avocet

AXILLARIES: the feathers at the base of the underside of the wing, the axilla.

Underside of wing

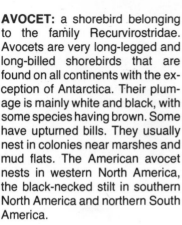

AVOCET: a shorebird belonging to the family Recurvirostridae. Avocets are very long-legged and long-billed shorebirds that are found on all continents with the exception of Antarctica. Their plumage is mainly white and black, with some species having brown. Some have upturned bills. They usually nest in colonies near marshes and mud flats. The American avocet nests in western North America, the black-necked stilt in southern North America and northern South America.

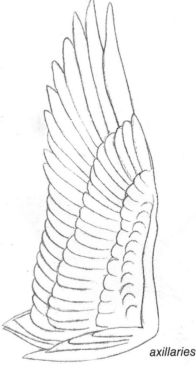

axillaries

B

Bee-eater

BABBLER: a member of the family Timaliidae. The 257 species of babblers inhabit Asia, Africa, and Australia. They are small- to medium-sized insectivorous birds that resemble warblers and thrushes. Most of them live in forests. Some are quite brightly colored, but most are dull or brownish. Their wings are rather short and they are poor flyers. Outside the breeding season they are usually seen in small flocks. Babblers were named for their rather vocal behavior. In the New World their ecological niche is taken by the *antbirds*.

BACHMAN, JOHN (1790–1874): American minister and amateur zoologist who had a warbler and a sparrow named after him.

Fluffy-backed tit babbler

Hummingbird balanced in flight.

BAIRD, SPENCER FULLERTON (1823–1887): American administrator and naturalist after whom Baird's sandpiper and Baird's sparrow are named. A warbler is named after his daughter Lucy.

BALANCE: to remain poised in a certain position. The labyrinth of the inner *ear* helps in maintaining the balance of a bird. Information from here as well as from the *eyes* and the *muscles* and joints is integrated in the cerebellum (hindbrain) and appropriate actions are then taken to maintain the balance. In *flight* this is done by the wing action as well as by angulation of the tail. The stability of a hovering hummingbird indicates the great efficacy of this system.

BANDING: the marking of an individual bird with a recognizable band for later identification. In Britain the preferred term for the practice is "ringing."

Bird banding was started in a systematic fashion by a Danish schoolteacher, Hans Christian C. Mortensen, in 1899. Bird banding spread very rapidly in Europe, somewhat more slowly in North America. Most bands in use are made of an aluminum alloy. A serial number and the name and address of the sponsoring institution are printed on the band. The band is placed around the leg of the bird, and the sponsoring institution keeps a record of each bird banded. When a band has been recovered, the time and place can be compared with the time and

Return of white storks banded in Denmark by H.C.C. Mortensen

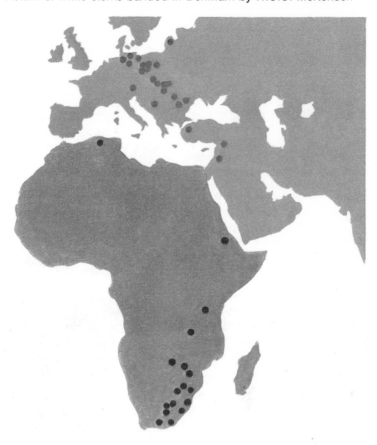

Two types of bands

place of banding. This method has made it possible to recognize individual birds and has been particularly valuable in studying their travel. As more and more stations for the capture, banding, and subsequent release of birds have been established, it has been possible to follow a number of individual birds through several recaptures. It is thus possible to gain insights into the pattern of *migration* as well as into the dynamics of specific *populations*.

The recovery rate for different species varies considerably due to several factors. Larger birds that are hunted have the highest recovery rate, whereas small birds of little economic value and retiring habits have the lowest (often under 1 per cent).

For special studies where individual visual recognition is necessary, different-colored plastic rings are used. This makes it possible to identify a given individual without having to capture it.

Other techniques of marking individual birds are neckbands, used particularly in swans, small metal plates clipped to the wings, used particularly in ducks, and painting of certain feathers for long-distance identification.

Hundreds of thousands of birds are marked annually and so many recoveries are now recorded that it has been necessary for several institutions to computerize the information for analysis.

BARB: a branch off the stem *feather*. The barbs and their *barbules* form the vane.

BARBET: a member of the family Capitonidae. Barbets are small, stocky birds with large heads and bills. The seventy-two species are found in the tropical forests of Central and South America, Africa, and southern Asia. They usually stay high in the treetops where they feed on insects and fruits. They nest in tree cavities, usually excavated by themselves. Most are solitary in habits.

Black-crowned barbet

Black-collared barbet

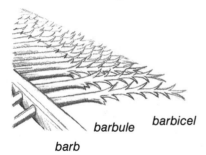

Interconnecting barbicels

barbule *barbicel*

barb

BARBICEL: a small branch off the *barbule*, which on the distal barbule is hooked, on the proximal barbule spoon-shaped. The distal barbicel off one barbule hooks into the proximal barbicel of the next barbule. In this way the smoothness and coherence of the vane of the *feather* is accomplished.

BARBULE: a branch off a *barb*, part of a *feather*.

BARN OWL: a member of the family Tytonidae. The ten species of barn owls are cosmopolitan, with the exception of Antarctica.

They are medium-sized *owls* that differ from typical owls by having heart-shaped, not round, facial disks.

BARROW, SIR JOHN (1764–1848): English administrator after whom Barrow's goldeneye is named.

BASIC PLUMAGE: used to denote the nonnuptial plumage when a species has more than one plumage per year, or the plumage in species where there is one only.

For other information see *Molt* and *Plumage*.

Barn owl

Bastard wing

rain by rolling over on their sides and holding the upper wing extended so that the flank is exposed.

Other types of behavior associated with feather maintenance are *preening*, *dusting*, and *anting*.

Pigeon bathing in rain

BASTARD WING: also called the alula. This term refers to the feathers attached to the first finger situated at the bend of the *wing*.

BATHING: the cleansing of the plumage with water. Bathing in water is performed by most species of birds and serves the purpose, together with oiling, of keeping the plumage intact. Most land birds bathe standing in shallow water, whereas most water birds bathe while swimming. The movements involved in bathing are often complex and elaborate. Some species, for instance pigeons, bathe in the

Thrush bathing

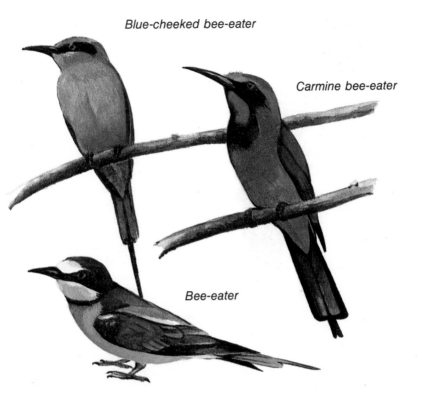

Blue-cheeked bee-eater

Carmine bee-eater

Bee-eater

BEE-EATER: a member of the family Meropidae. These brilliant-colored, medium-sized birds are widespread in the warmer parts of the Old World. They have long wings and tails and long, slender bills, all adaptions to their habit of catching larger insects, bees and wasps in particular, in the air. Bee-eaters are usually gregarious in their habits and most nest in colonies. They nest in burrows made in banks. There are twenty-four species of bee-eaters.

BEHAVIOR: in its broadest sense, the response of an organism to external as well as internal stimuli.

Behavior in birds, as in other animals, consists of a large variety of reactions that make it possible for the individual to survive and reproduce. This behavior can either be caused by *instinct* or obtained through *imprinting* or *learning*. For the individual's survival it involves such things as feeding habits (see *food*), *drinking*, *feather* mainte-nance, as well as *aggression* and *dominance*. Behavioral patterns involved in reproduction concern *territory* (which may be defended by *singing*), *display*, *courtship*, *nest* building, *incubation*, and the feeding of the young.

Black-throated butcher-bird

BELL, JOHN GRAHAM (1812–1889): American taxidermist. Bell's vireo is named after him.

BELL MAGPIE: a member of the family Cracticidae. The ten species of bell magpies inhabit semi-open country in Australia and New Guinea. They are medium-sized to large social birds that live mainly on insects.

BENDIRE, CHARLES EMIL (1836–1897): German-born American soldier and amateur ornithologist after whom the Bendire's thrasher is named.

BERGMANN'S RULE: the principle that the body size within a species tends to be larger in the cooler part of its range.

BEWICK, THOMAS (1753–1828): English wood engraver and naturalist after whom the Bewick's wren is named.

BIBLICAL BIRDS: the species of birds mentioned in the Bible are relatively few considering the richness of the avifauna of the Near East. Most of those named are either very large birds (ostriches, pelicans, birds of prey) or very common ones (swallows, house sparrows, pigeons). Most are mentioned in the lists of unclean animals. However, the spectacular arrival of migrating quails in the fall is also described.

BILL: the projecting jaws with their horny coverings. The bill consists of two major parts, the upper mandible attached to the facial bones and the lower mandible attached to the underside of the skull with two joints. On the upper bill are found the two nostrils, which are variable in both shape and form and may even be lacking. Both upper and lower mandibles have horny coverings that can regenerate as the bill becomes worn. In some species, for instance puffins, this horny coverage is very large and colorful in the breeding season, but is replaced in winter by a much smaller, blackish covering. When the embryo develops in the egg, a small, sharp egg tooth is found on the upper part of the tip of the upper mandible. This egg tooth is used for cutting through the eggshell when the young hatch. It is shed shortly after hatching.

The shape of the bill of various birds is clearly adapted to the *food* obtained. Hawks have a strong hooked bill that easily tears meat. Herons have a long, sharp bill with which they can grasp fish. Seed-eating birds have heavy conical bills for cracking seeds. The bills of most shorebirds are long

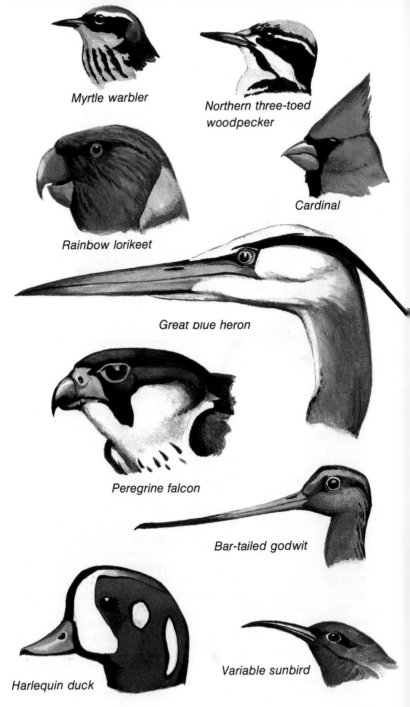

Myrtle warbler

Northern three-toed
woodpecker

Cardinal

Rainbow lorikeet

Great blue heron

Peregrine falcon

Bar-tailed godwit

Harlequin duck

Variable sunbird

and slender for probing into mud. Insectivorous birds usually have small, slender bills. Ducks have wide bills with which they are able to grasp plants or smaller animals. Many bills show a high degree of adaptation. Extreme examples are the very long hook at the tip of the Everglades kite's bill, which is used for extracting snails, the complicated sifting mechanism of the flamingo's bill, which is used upside down when feeding, and the huge bill of the pelican used for grabbing fish.

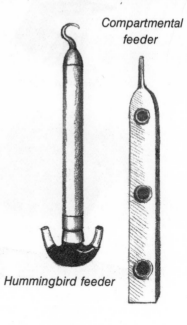

Compartmental feeder

Hummingbird feeder

Everglades kite

BINOMINAL SYSTEM: the system of *nomenclature* used by *Linnaeus* in his *Systema Naturae*. In this way each species is identified by two names: the first one refers to the *genus*, the second identifies the *species* within the genus.

BIRD: a member of the class Aves. Birds can be distinguished from all other animals by having *feathers*. Most birds are capable of *flight*, their forelimbs being especially adapted to this function. With the loss of the forelimbs as manipulative organs the mouth developed into a specialized tool taking many different shapes and forms (see *bill*).

BIRD FEEDER: an apparatus containing food available to birds. Most bird feeders are simple trays with a cover, situated above the ground to protect the birds from predators and discourage rodents from eating the food. Some bird feeders are more elaborate or specialized. Bird feeders are most successful in attracting birds at times when food is scarce.

BIRDHOUSE: an artificial nesting site for birds. Birdhouses or nest boxes are mainly used by birds that nest in natural cavities such as titmice, starlings, and bluebirds. With increasingly efficient husbandry of forests and woods, natural tree cavities are becoming scarce in many areas and birdhouses can help in maintaining or increasing the population of the hole-nesting species.

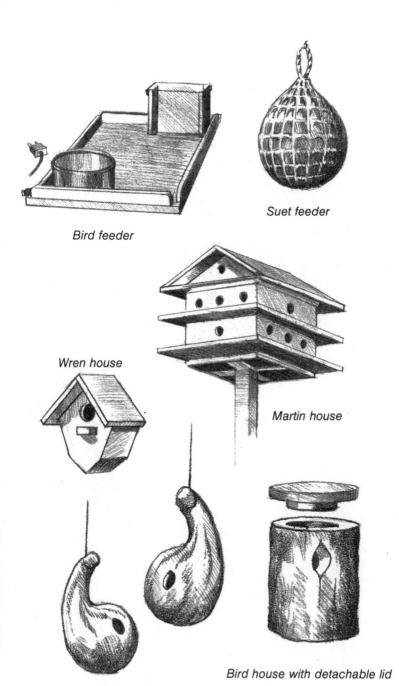

Bird feeder

Suet feeder

Wren house

Martin house

Bird houses made of gourds

Bird house with detachable lid

Count Raggi's bird of paradise

King of Saxony bird of paradise

BIRD OF PARADISE: a member of the family Paradisaeidae. The forty species of birds of paradise are found in New Guinea and neighboring areas. They are small to medium-sized forest-dwelling birds. The males have extremely colorful plumage with elongated, curved, and bent feathers. The females, however, are dull-colored brown or gray without ornamental feathers. The courtship display of birds of paradise is very elaborate and involves a great variety of positions (among which may be hanging upside down) in which their spectacular plumes are exhibited to the female. Birds of paradise live mainly on fruits and on insects. They are solitary in habits.

26

BIRD OF PREY: a member of the order of Falconiformes. This order includes the *accipiters*, *buzzards*, *eagles*, *falcons*, *harriers*, *hawks*, *ospreys*, *secretary birds*, and *vultures*. Sometimes the term "birds of prey" is used in a wider sense to include the *owls*, members of the order Strigiformes.

BIRD WATCHING: usually used to denote observation of birds in the field. It is most often applied to the amateur, while the serious study of birds is termed *ornithology*. However, a vast amount of research has been done, and a large quantity of material for research collected, by amateurs and integrated into the accumulated knowledge of birds.

The past forty years have seen a marked increase in the interest in wildlife in general and birds in particular. From being a pursuit of the individualist, bird watching has to a large degree changed into an organized recreational pursuit in which vast amounts of knowledge are assembled. These observations, which could not conveivably be made by one person alone, are then analyzed to give us a clearer understanding of the life of birds. This development, which is principally the work of various organizations, whose members include amateurs as well as professionals, has resulted in a tremendous increase in our knowledge. It is an illustration of the beneficial effect of collaboration between diverse groups with similar interests.

BITTERN: a member of the subfamily Botaurinae. Bitterns are closely related to *herons*, but in general have shorter necks and legs and more cryptic coloration. Bitterns are medium-sized to rather large marsh birds. They are much more secretive in behavior than herons. They inhabit all continents with the exception of Antarctica. The large bitterns have characteristic booming calls that are mainly given at dusk. Bitterns are solitary in habits. Least and American bitterns occur in North America.

American bittern

BLACKBURN, ASHTON (17?–1780): Scottish bird collector after whom the Blackburnian warbler is named.

BLOOD: the fluid that carries oxygen and nutrients necessary for metabolism to all parts of the body through the *vascular system*. The avian blood differs from mammalian blood by containing larger red cells that are oval in shape. Otherwise blood of birds closely resembles that of mammals, including man.

BONAPARTE, CHARLES LUCIEN (1803–1857): a nephew of Napoleon I and an amateur ornithologist after whom the Bonaparte's gull is named. The Zenaida dove is named after his wife, Princess Zénaïde.

BOOBY: common name used for some members of the family Sulidae, closely related to the *gannets*.

BOOMING GROUND: the display ground used by the greater prairie chicken of North America, where males gather to display for the females.

BOTTERI, MATEO (1808–1877): Dalmatian collector after whom the Botteri's sparrow is named.

Greater prairie chicken

28

Satin bowerbird

BOWERBIRD: a member of the family Ptilonorhynchidae. The seventeen species of bowerbirds inhabit the forests of New Guinea and northern Australia. The males build elaborate stages decorated with different-colored articles and in different shapes for their display and courtship. Bowerbirds are often divided into three subgroups, namely platform builders, maypole builders, and avenue builders. Bowerbirds are medium-sized, omnivorous passerines that are solitary in habits.

BRAILING: a way of making a bird flightless by binding the wing so that it cannot be extended.

BRAIN: part of the central *nervous system*.

BRANDT, JOHANN FRIEDRICH VON (1802–1879): German-Russian zoologist after whom the Brandt's cormorant is named.

BREEDING: all activities associated with reproduction. During the *breeding season* most birds set up a *territory* and a mate is obtained through *courtship*. The *nest* is usually placed within the territory. When the *eggs* are laid, *incubation* starts. After a variable amount of time the *young* hatch and are then cared for for a variable period of time until they become independent. The success of breeding (the number of eggs hatched, the number of young surviving) clearly has an influence on the bird *population* and is influenced by many factors, such as weather, availability of food, and man's activities, including the spraying of poisons, *insecticides* in particular. (See also *reproductive system*.)

BREEDING SEASON: the time of year at which *breeding* takes place for a certain species in a certain area. Both the time and the length of the season vary from species to species and even within the same species.

Most birds have a well-defined season, the time of which is determined by the physiological state of the bird and the availability of food in a given environment. The species nesting in the North Temperate and Arctic zones usually breed in the spring or early summer. Their physiological readiness for breeding is influenced by the increasing length of days. This has been proven experimentally by exposing caged birds to varying lengths of daylight, thus manipulating the time of breeding. In other areas the length of day appears to be of minor or no importance in determining the breeding season. In areas of the tropics where rainfall is seasonal the breeding cycle of most species can be correlated to the rain. In areas like Australia where rainfall is unpredictable and irregular the many species of birds appear to respond to the actual rainfall itself.

Most species will breed once a year, but many of the smaller *passerines* are able to rear more than one brood per season. Some of the larger species, condors and albatrosses in particular, cannot breed more often than every other year, as their young grow so slowly that the process of breeding takes more than one year.

BREWER, THOMAS MAYO (1814–1880): American physician and publisher after whom a blackbird and a sparrow are named.

BRIDLING: a facial pattern that resembles a bridle; for instance, in the bridled titmouse.

BROADBILL: a member of the family Eurylaimidae. The fourteen species of broadbills inhabit the tropical part of the Old World from Africa to the Philippines. They are most numerous in the Indonesian

Bridled tit

region. Broadbills are medium-sized forest birds with short, rounded wings and a very wide, flat bill. Most live on insects. Broadbills build elaborate pear-shaped nests suspended from branches.

BROODING: the act by the parent bird of sitting on the young to protect them from adverse environmental effects, particularly cold. Most birds brood their young for rather long periods of time

Long-tailed broadbill

Roseate tern brooding young

immediately after hatching, but then decrease the amount of time spent in brooding as the young grow. Parents often brood their young during rain, and on hot days they protect their young from the effect of the direct sun by brooding.

BROOD PATCH: one or several areas on the underside of the adult bird where the feathers are shed and the skin becomes swollen at the time of *incubation*. Brood patches are richly supplied with blood, raising the skin temperature considerably, thus facilitating the transfer of heat from the parent bird to the egg. For unknown reasons some birds appear not to have brood patches.

BUFFON, GEORGE LOUIS LE-CLERC, COMTE DE (1707–1788): French naturalist and author of the famous *Histoire naturelle* which was the first book to present all facts of natural history in an intelligible form.

Brood patch

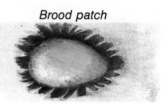

BULBUL: a member of the family Pycnonotidae. The 119 species of bulbuls inhabit Africa and southern Asia to the Philippines. They are usually found in forests or brush-lands. Outside the breeding season they are quite gregarious. Bulbuls are medium-sized birds with rather dull colorations. They live on insects, fruits, and buds.

Terrestrial bulbul

Slender bulbul

31

Varied bunting

Snow bunting

Painted bunting

BULLER, SIR WALTER LAWRY (1838–1906): New Zealand lawyer and ornithologist.

BULWER, JAMES (1794–1879): English clergyman and amateur naturalist after whom the Bulwer's petrel is named.

BUNTING: a member of the subfamily Emberizinae, closely related to the *sparrows*, *finches*, *cardinals*, and *grosbeaks*. All belong to the family Fringillidae. In America the term is also used for colorful birds more closely related to the cardinals than to the Old World buntings.

The Old World buntings are mainly seed-eating, ground-dwelling, sparrowlike birds, living primarily on seeds. Two Old World species, the snow bunting and the Lapland longspur, occur in North America. The New World members of the subfamily are described at the entry for *sparrow*.

BUSTARD: a member of the family Otidae. The twenty-three species of bustards are large, long-legged and long-necked ground-dwelling birds found in open lands of the Old World. They are brown, black or white in colors. Bustards are often met with in flocks.

BUTEO: a member of the subfamily Buteoninae, also called true *hawks* and *eagles*.

BUTTON QUAIL: synonymous with *hemipode*.

BUZZARD: the British name for *buteos* and *hawks*. In North America the term is often used for the *New World vultures*.

Chickadee

CAGE BIRD: a small bird kept in captivity. Common cage birds are budgerigars from Australia, mynas from India, canaries from the Canary Islands, various finches and weaverbirds, as well as several species of parrots and doves. Birds are kept in cages for several reasons, the beauty of the plumage and song being the most common. Myna birds and several parrots are often kept because of their ability in mimicry. Most cage birds are herbivorous, of which granivorous ones are the kinds easiest to keep.

CALAMUS: the nude part of the shaft of a *feather*.

CALL NOTE: vocalization associated with maintenance behavior (as opposed to *singing*, which is concerned with reproductive behavior). Virtually all birds have call notes by which they are able to communicate information to other members of their kind. Many species have different call notes to serve different functions. The alarm call is usually very short and penetrating and difficult to localize. This is of obvious ad-

Cage birds

Budgerigar

Indian hill mynah

Masked lovebird

Gouldian finch

33

vantage to the bird calling since the predator will have difficulty localizing the source. Many species have different alarm calls for different types of dangers. Call notes are also important in keeping flocks together. It appears that call notes are inborn, as is the response to a given call note. Thus the newborn young will respond appropriately to their parents' alarm call. Although call notes are relatively simple compared to song, they vary from species to species and are thus helpful in establishing identification. This is particularly true if one wants to record night migrants, as they are invisible but easily heard.

CAPON: a castrated domestic fowl with particularly tender meat.

CAPRIMULGIFORMES: an order containing the families of *frogmouths*, *goatsuckers*, *oilbirds*, *owlet frogmouths*, and *potoos*.

CARACARA: a member of the subfamily Daptriinae, closely related to the *falcons*. Caracaras are large, broad-winged, long-legged birds of prey that primarily live on carrion. They are limited in their distribution to the New World, and most are found in South America. The caracara reaches from the north to southwestern United States and to Florida.

CARDINAL: a member of the subfamily Pyrrhuloxiinae, which belongs to the family of New World seedeaters (Fringillidae). The group consists of small- to medium-sized birds, usually brilliantly colored. They are limited to the New World, where they inhabit brushlands and woods. The best-known North American representative of the group is the cardinal with its brilliant red colors. Other members of Pyrrhuloxia include the rose-breasted and black-headed gros-

Caracara

Cardinal male and female

beak, blue grosbeak, indigo bunting, azuli bunting, and painted and varied buntings.

CARRYING: Birds usually carry objects from one place to another either in their bill or in their feet. However, there are examples of birds carrying their young between their legs, for instance in the case of the American woodcock. Some species of *sandgrouse* carry water to their young in their breast feathers. Ducks and other waterfowl often carry their young on their backs when swimming. Some penguins carry their eggs on the top of their feet.

King penguins carry their eggs.

35

Casque

CASQUE: the enlargement of the bill in front of the head or on the head of certain species like the hornbills and cassowaries.

CASSIN, JOHN (1813–1869): American businessman and naturalist after whom an auklet, a kingbird, a finch and a sparrow are named.

CASSOWARY: a member of the family Casuariidae. Three species of these very large ostrichlike birds live in New Guinea and northern Australia. They are generally black with a naked head that carries a casque. They are forest dwellers.

CASUARIIFORMES: an order containing the families of *cassowaries* and *emus*.

CATBIRD: term used for several different and unrelated species in various parts of the world. In North America the name is used for a small blackish bird related to thrushes.

Australian cassowary

CENSUS: a term often used synonymously with *count*, although it should probably be restricted to the estimation of a breeding *population*. Census-taking is of great importance, particularly in the management of wildlife. Various methods of census-taking are employed, including nest counting and counts in which singing males in a certain habitat are enumerated. The methods employed are dependent on the exact purpose of the census as well as on local conditions.

CERE: the soft covering at the base of the upper mandible, present in such birds as doves.

Cere

CETTI, FRANCOIS (1726–1780): Italian priest and naturalist of the Mediterranean region.

CHARADRIIFORMES: a large order of shorebirds containing the families of *auks*, *avocets*, *crab plovers*, *gulls* and *terns*, *jacanas*, *jaegers*, *oystercatchers*, *painted snipes*, *phalaropes*, *plovers*, *sandpipers*, *seedsnipes*, *sheathbills*, *skimmers*, and *thick-knees*.

CHAT: a name used for several different and unrelated species in various parts of the world. In North America the name is applied to some members of the New World warblers.

CHICKADEE: a name for some North American *titmice*.

CIRCADIAN: having a daily biological rhythm.

CLARK, WILLIAM (1770–1838): American soldier and explorer of the West after whom the Clark's nutcracker is named.

CLASS: a category used in taxonomy. All birds belong to the class Aves and have developed from the class Reptilia.

CLASSIFICATION: the grouping of objects or phenomena into different categories. Most modern classifications of birds are based on evolutionary concepts. *Taxonomy* has such classification as its purpose.

CLAW: one of the horny appendages of the toes or fingers. The claws on the toes of birds vary from rudimentary to very large, as for instance in birds of prey. Claws are found on the wings of *secretary birds*, *screamers*, and *hoatzins*.

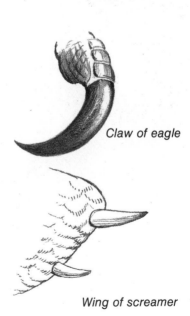

Claw of eagle

Wing of screamer

CLEIDOIC: denoting the living conditions in the enclosed system of an *egg*.

CLIMATE: the weather conditions over an extended period of time, including seasonal changes.

Climate has a profound influence on the distribution of plant and animal species. Most species are adapted to particular types of climate.

CLINE: a population of a species showing changes according to the geographic distribution.

CLIPPING: the cutting of the primary feathers of one wing of a captive bird to inhibit its flight.

CLOACA: the combined lower opening of the *alimentary tract,* the *urinary system,* and the *reproductive system* in birds.

CLUTCH: the complete set of eggs laid by one female. Clutch size varies tremendously in different species of birds, and even within the same species differences are found. Each species, however, has a tendency to lay a certain number of eggs in its clutch. Many species lay but one egg, whereas some, such as the partridge, may have a clutch as large as fifteen.

COCK: a male bird; used specifically for the domestic fowl.

Black grouse with its clutch

COCKATOO: a member of the subfamily Kakatoeinae, members of the family of *parrots*. Cockatoos are large parrots with a long crest.

COLIIFORMES: an order containing the single family of *mousebirds*.

COLLARED HEMIPODE: the single member of the family Pedionomidae. The collared hemipode is very similar to the hemipodes, and is found in Australia. It is a small, quail-like, brown-and-black bird.

COLONY: a group of birds nesting in close proximity.

Collared hemipode

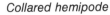

Sulphur-crested cockatoo

feathers causing either interference, which gives iridescent colors, or the scattering of light waves, giving rise to noniridescent colors.

The many different colors found in feathers are produced by either pigmentary or structural colors or by combinations of both.

The different colorations of birds serve two main functions, namely concealment and recognition.

COLOR: the quality of light in regard to the visual sensation produced. Birds are among the most colorful of animals. The colors of the feathers are produced in two ways: pigmentary colors, the most common, are produced by the incorporation in the feathers of colored elements—melanin, which is black or brown; carotenoids responsible for red and orange colors; as well as porphyrins and several other types of pigment. Structural colors are caused by specific physical features of the

COLUMBIFORMES: an order containing the families of *pigeons* and *sandgrouse*. The dodo also belonged to this order.

COMB: a naked, fleshy, usually bright-colored structure situated on the top of the head.

COMFORT MOVEMENTS: the various movements of ruffling, shaking, stretching, etc., performed by many birds to put the feathers in order.

Andean condor

CONDOR: one of the two largest members of the *New World vultures*.

CONSERVATION: measures taken to protect and possibly enhance animals, plants, or other natural resources. In regard to birds, several measures for their conservation are employed. Legal protection in the form of hunting laws are used almost universally. Sanctuaries of varying sizes, to protect either a special habitat or a specific bird, have been set up. As land utilization by man has developed it has become clear that many of these sanctuaries are too small and are not capable of supporting an entire ecological system. The improvement of existing habitats and the creation of suitable artificial habitats are playing an increasing role as we have gained knowledge of the destructive effects of man. These measures include the creation of lakes and ponds as well as planting of cover and supplementing of nest holes by putting up nest boxes. The problem of protecting wildlife from pollution remains largely unsolved. Legislation banning the use of certain *insecticides*, is, however, increasingly widespread.

It is clear that the conservation measures presently employed are not sufficient to protect wildlife in a satisfactory way. Much basic research and experimentation are necessary, as is a broader public understanding of the problems of an ever-dwindling wildlife.

CONSPECIFIC: denoting that two or several forms of subspecies belong to the same species.

CONTOUR FEATHER: a *feather* that is visible on the outer surface of the body.

CONTROL OF BIRDS: the attempt to keep a species within certain limits in regard to population size. Control measures are taken when certain species become pests. Attempts have been made to control the number of birds near airports, in central parts of cities, and under special circumstances where large concentrations may cause harm to agricultural products. By and large, most control measures have been rather unsuccessful, although many different approaches have been taken. These various measures include shooting, poisoning, frightening with alarm calls, the use of falcons, the use of electric wiring, and the destruction of eggs.

CONVERGENCE: evolution from two unrelated sources in a similar fashion as an adaption to the same environment.

COOK, JAMES (1728–1779): English sailor who explored the South Pacific in particular. A petrel is named after him.

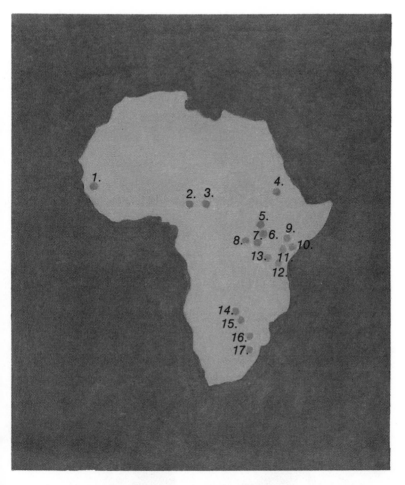

1. Niocolo-koba	10. Tsavo
2. Waza	11. Amboseli
3. Zakouma	12. Ngorongoro
4. Dinder	13. Serengeti
5. Nimule	14. Kafue
6. Murchison Falls	15. Wankie
7. Queen Elizabeth	16. Kruger
8. Albert	17. Umfolozi
9. Nairobi	

COOPER, WILLIAM (1798–1864): American zoologist after whom a hawk is named.

COOT: any of a group of birds closely related to the *rails* and *gallinules*.

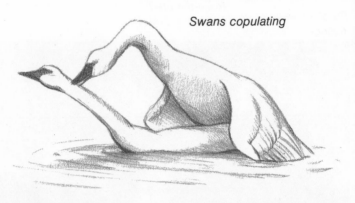
Swans copulating

COPULATION: uniting in the sexual act. In birds copulation is performed with one bird, usually the male, mounting the other. The tails are held to the side so that the *cloaca* are approximated. Sperm is released by the male and fertilizes the egg. In most cases copulation takes place on the ground, but it may take place on a perch, in the water, or even in the air (as among the *swifts*).

CORACIIFORMES: an order containing the families of *bee-eaters*, *cuckoo-rollers*, *ground rollers*, *hoopoes*, *hornbills*, *kingfishers*, *motmots*, *rollers*, *todies*, and *wood hoopoes*.

CORMORANT: a member of the family Phalacrocoracidae, related to the *pelicans*, *anhingas*, and *gannets*. Cormorants are medium-sized to large swimming birds, usually adorned with a crest.

Olivaceous cormorants

Purple-breasted cotinga

Rose-throated becard

Cock-of-the-rock

Most are black or black and white. They may be found in both fresh and salt water. They live on fish pursued and caught under water, and are colonial in their nesting habits.

CORY, CHARLES BARNEY (1857–1921): American ornithologist after whom a shearwater is named.

COSMOPOLITAN: distributed through most of the geographical regions of the world.

COTINGA: a member of the family Cotingidae. Members of this family are found in the New World only, particularly in the tropical regions. They are small to medium-sized, very colorful birds that inhabit forests. The most spectacular of the cotingas is the cock of the rock found in northeastern South America. The only North American representative of the family is the rose-throated becard found in the Southwest. Cotingas are related to the *tyrant flycatchers*.

COUES, ELLIOT (1842–1899): American physician and naturalist after whom a flycatcher is named. Grace's warbler is named after his sister.

COUNT: a method of attempting to evaluate the size of a population in a given area. Whereas the term *census* mainly refers to a breeding population, count is used in reference to nonbreeding birds. In several areas systematic counts of birds in a specific locality and at a specific time have been organized. It is thus possible to estimate annual changes in population size. Most famous is the Christmas count conducted in North America. Waterfowl counts are made in most parts of the world.

COURSER: a member of the subfamily Cursoriinae, which together with the pratincoles form the family Glareolidae. They are medium-sized ploverlike birds with pointed bills. The sixteen species are found in Eurasia, Africa and Australia.

Cream-colored courser

COURTSHIP: the activities related to attracting and maintaining a mate. Courtship in birds is often very elaborate and involves the *pair* formation during which the normal aggressive behavior toward members of the same species is decreased toward the mate and replaced by acceptance. During courtship birds *display*, which appears to facilitate the establishment of a pair bond. Singing plays an important part in the courtship of many birds. In some species the feeding of one mate by the other forms an integral part of the courtship. This is, for instance, the case with terns and some finches. Pursuit in flight is also often part of courtship display.

Malay argus pheasant

Gannet

Ruddy duck

Ruff

Sage grouse

Great crested grebe

Frigate bird

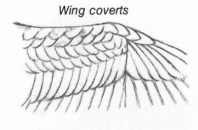
Wing coverts

COVERT: one of the contour feathers that cover the bases of the wing and tail feathers as well as the outer ear.

CRAB PLOVER: the single member of the family Dromadidae, related to other shorebirds. The crab plover is a handsome white-and-black, medium-sized, long-legged shorebird found along the northern coast of the Indian Ocean. It is gregarious in its habits.

CRANE: a member of the family Gruidae. The fourteen species of cranes inhabit Eurasia, North America, and Australia. They are very large, long-legged and long-necked, storklike birds with largely white, gray, and black plumages. Cranes inhabit open plains and marshes. North American representatives are the widespread sandhill crane and the larger, almost extinct whooping crane.

CRAVERI, FREDERICO (1815–1890): Italian chemist after whom the Craveri's murrelet is named.

CREEPER: a member of the family Certhiidae. The six species of creepers inhabit woodlands of North America, Europe, Asia and Northern Africa. They are small, brown passerines which find their insect food in crevices of bark or on rocks.

CRESTED SWIFT: a member of the family Hemiprognidae. The three species inhabit southern Asia where they are found in flocks at forest edges. They resemble swifts closely but are crested.

Crab plover

Chough

Fish crow

CROW: any of the members of the family Corvidae. Belonging to the family are the *jays* and *magpies*, as well as the nutcrackers, choughs, and typical crows. Nutcrackers are medium-sized birds, one inhabiting coniferous forests of the Palearctic region; the other, Clark's nutcracker, inhabiting western North America. Choughs are medium-sized black crows inhabiting mountainous areas of Eurasia. The typical crows are medium-sized to large, usually black birds with strong bills. North American species include the common raven, white-necked raven, common crow, northwestern crow and fish crow.

CRYPTIC: denoting behavioral coloration that helps concealment.

CUCKOO: a member of the family Cuculidae. Members of this family are cosmopolitan in their distribution. They are medium-sized birds with long tails that are usually quite dull-colored. The most famous of the cuckoos are the parasitic members of the family, the so-called parasitic cuckoos, which lay eggs in the nests of other birds who will then care for the eggs and young of the cuckoo. Best known of these parasitic birds is the cuckoo found throughout most of Eurasia. Its characteristic call

Yellow-billed cuckoo

47

has given rise to the name of the family. The two North American cuckoos, the black-billed and yellow-billed cuckoos, are non-parasitic. In North America are also found the *anis* and the road-runners. Roadrunners are large, long-legged and long-tailed ground-dwelling birds that live on insects, snakes, and lizards. Another subfamily, the coucals, is distributed over Africa, southern Asia, and Australia.

CUCKOO-ROLLER: the one species belonging to the family Leptosomatidae. Cuckoo-rollers are medium-sized, crowlike forest dwellers found in Madagascar.

Cuckoo-roller

Cuckoo shrike

CUCKOO SHRIKE: a member of the family Campephagidae. The seventy species are divided into two groups, the cuckoo shrikes proper, which are rather drab-colored, and the minivets, which are mainly red and black. Cuckoo shrikes are medium-sized, somewhat thrushlike forest dwellers of the tropical parts of the Old World.

CUCULIFORMES: an order which contains the families of *cuckoos* and *touracos*.

CULMEN: the highest central ridge of the upper mandible of the *bill*.

CURASSOW: a member of the family Cracidae. This New World family of medium-sized to large pheasantlike birds includes thirty-eight species. They are forest birds of the tropical South American jungle. One species, the chachalaca, reaches the southwestern part of the United States.

CURLEW: one of several species of rather large, brown, long-legged shorebirds with decurved bills. They belong to the family of *sandpipers*.

CYGNET: the young of a *swan*.

Cygnet

D

Blue-winged teal

Woodpecker finch

DANCING GROUND: the display ground of the sharp-tailed grouse, which inhabits the northwestern prairies of North America.

DARTER: alternative name for the *anhinga*.

DARWIN, CHARLES ROBERT (1809–1882): English naturalist who described the theory of evolution in his *Origin of Species*, published in 1859, causing a revolution in zoology. He was the naturalist on the H.M.S. *Beagle* during its four-year-long circumnavigation of the earth. Several birds and other animals are named after him.

DARWIN'S FINCH: alternative name for the *Galápagos finch*.

DEATH RATE: see *mortality*.

Sharp-tailed grouse

Various types of decoys

DECOY: 1—an artificial, clipped, or tame bird used to attract other birds, usually for the purpose of shooting from a blind. The use of artificial decoys has been particularly prevalent in the United States. Although most decoys used are renderings of ducks or geese, other species like shorebirds, crows, and owls are used. In eastern North America the creation of decoys has developed into an art form, and decoys made by especially skillful hunters are prized collector's items. Today most decoys are made of plastic.

2—a large trap at the side of a lake used for catching ducks.

DIGESTION: the process of mechanical and chemical breakdown of food items to simpler, absorbable nutrients. This process takes place in the *alimentary canal*.

DIMORPHISM: the presence in a given population of two different and genetically determined forms. By far the most common type of dimorphism is *sexual dimorphism*. Examples of nonsexual dimorphism are the reddish egret, which occurs in a red and a white form, and the rough-legged, ferruginous, red-tailed, Swanson's, Harlan's, and short-tailed hawks, all of which occur in a dark and a light phase. More than two phases may occur.

Parasitic jaeger

dark phase

light phase

Red-tailed hawk

ringed phase Rt.

Screech owl

Common murre

red phase

grey phase

Dipper

North American dipper

DIPPER: a member of the family Cinclidae. The four species of dippers inhabit Europe and Asia, as well as the western mountains of both North and South America. Dippers are medium-sized, chubby, short-tailed passerines. Their plumage is rather plain. Dippers live by rivers and lakes where they seek their food under water by running along the bottom. They are solitary in their habits.

DISEASE: an impairment of the normal state of a living organism or any of its parts that influences the performance of vital functions adversely.

Disease is common among birds, but our knowledge of these diseases is limited. The range of diseases closely resembles that known in man himself. Parasitic diseases caused by both *ectoparasites* and *endoparasites* are extremely common. Most birds are infested with such ectoparasites as flies and mites and such endoparasites as worms. It appears, however, that only with overwhelming infestation is the health of the bird seriously impaired. Infectious diseases among birds, particularly domestic kinds, are the best known. Protozoan infections, particularly by plasmodia that cause malaria, are extremely common. Fungal diseases are widespread and the occasional transmittance of these diseases from domestic fowl or pigeons has caused some concern. Bacterial diseases such as tuberculosis and pasteurellosis are also found among birds. Viral diseases like encephalitis, plague and pox, psittacosis (which occasionally affects man), and even upper respiratory tract infections resembling colds are not uncommon.

Of the noninfectious diseases, poisoning can cause great losses among birds. Lead poisoning, which may occur in waterfowl frequenting heavily hunted lakes and marshes, can cause serious losses in the waterfowl population. The effects of insecticides can be extremely detrimental. Botulism caused by the toxin produced by bacteria may cause severe losses, particularly among waterfowl. It is, for instance, estimated that 3 million birds died at Great Salt Lake during an outbreak in 1929.

Deficiency diseases in the form of specific vitamin deficiency or plain malnutrition are extremely common. The affected animal is also more prone to succumb from otherwise less harmful infectious diseases.

Tumors, benign and malignant, are found in birds and even leukemia has been discovered.

DISPERSION: the separation of individuals in space, particularly in regard to *population*, in which case *territory* plays an important role.

DISPLACEMENT BEHAVIOR: apparent transfer of activity to an irrelevant act.

Displacement behavior is extremely common among birds. Such behavior as, for instance, preening may occur in situations where a bird is frightened but not frightened enough to take flight. It may also occur when the bird is suddenly faced with a previously unknown situation.

DISPLAY: the ritualized movements used in communication between inviduals.

Faced with a mirror image birds may revert to irrelevant behavior like preening.

Display plays an extremely important role in birds. Several types have been described. Threat display is usually used between rivals. Submissive display is obviously related to threat display. Sexual display is used between mates or potential mates in both *pair* formation, in courtship and the establishment of the pair bond. Special types of display are often associated with *copulation* and in distracting predators.

Twelve-wired bird of paradise displaying

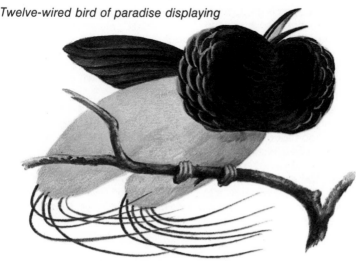

Distraction display by killdeer

The physical movements of display are often accompanied by vocalization, and *singing* serves a similar function to several types of display. Certain species like ruffs, several kinds of *grouse*, and some *birds of paradise* perform communal display where several males congregate (see *lek*).

DISTRACTION DISPLAY: the display of a parent bird attempting to lure predators away from eggs and young. Distraction display is widespread among birds, but is particularly common among ground-dwelling species. Several species of ducks and shorebirds perform during this display in such a fashion that the observer might think the bird was incapacitated by a broken wing or leg, so-called *injury feigning*. Another type of distraction display is the so-called mammal simulation, where the bird by crouching and running very fast, rather than taking flight, resembles a small rodent trying to escape in the grass. Both types of display attract the attention of the predator to the adult bird, which is capable of flight, and detract it from its progeny.

DISTRIBUTION: the total range of a species, genus, family, etc.

The distribution of a given species is limited by a multitude of factors such as *climate*, geography, and the origin of the species. The study of the distribution of animals is called zoogeography.

DIURNAL: active during the daytime.

DIVER: alternative name for the *loon*.

DIVING PETREL: a member of the family Pelecanoididae. The four species of diving petrels are restricted to the oceans surrounding Antarctica. They are small- to medium-sized, black-and-white birds that although closely related to the *storm petrels*, have a superficial resemblance to the unrelated

54

smaller *auks*, an example of *convergence*. They obtain their food by diving under water, and nest in burrows and holes in the ground.

DOMESTICATED BIRD: a bird whose life cycle and maintenance are controlled by man, particularly for the purpose of economic gain. The domestic pigeon, a descendant of the rock dove, is probably the oldest domesticated bird, reaching as far back as 3000 B.C., when it was in use in the Middle East. The domestic fowl, descended from the red jungle fowl, became domesticated in southern Asia about 2000 B.C. The domestic goose is descended from two different species, the greylag goose and the Chinese goose. They were both domesticated at least before 500 B.C. The domestic duck, which has the mallard as its ancestor, was probably originally domesticated in the Far East. The peacock originated in

Common diving pètrel

India. In North America the *turkey* and the Muscovy duck were both domesticated in pre-Columbian times. Other birds that have been domesticated are the *ostrich* (for its feathers) and a species of *cormorant,* which was used for fishing in Oriental countries.

Turkey

55

DOMINANCE: the commanding position in an order of forcefulness. Dominance among birds refers to the relative predictability of the outcome of a fight between two individual birds. Thus a male fighting within its own territory will almost always be dominant over an intruder. In several species of birds living in flocks, as well as among caged birds, hierarchies are formed, so-called *pecking orders*. In such cases one individual will be dominant over all other individuals in the group, another will be dominant over all but the first, etc. Although fights for a social position in such a hierarchy occur, the order, once established, is not often changed.

DOVE: any of various members of the family of *pigeons*.

DOWN: a special type of feather, usually hidden from view by the *contour feathers*.

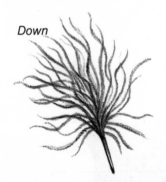
Down

DRAKE: a male duck.

DRIFT: the displacement of a migrating bird by the wind. Drift is often the cause of species occurring far from their normal range.

DRINKING: the ingestion of water. The process of drinking varies among different species. Essentially there are two ways in which water is swallowed, either by filling the bill and throwing the head upward, or, as in *pigeons*, *sand grouse*, and *hemipodes*, by sucking the water from a pool. The demand for water varies from species to species, as well as in the same individual, depending on loss of water. Certain species living in deserts require very little water, an adaption enabling them to survive extended periods of drought.

Doves suck up water when drinking, most other species throw their heads upwards to swallow water.

Tennessee warbler

Large raquet-tailed drongo

absorbed. White material present in the droppings of many species consists of uric acid and salts. The color of droppings is also influenced by the food eaten and often reflects digested chemicals that have passed through the *alimentary canal*. The droppings of the young of many passerine birds are enclosed in a gelatinous sac, enabling the parent bird to remove the droppings, the accumulation of which would make the nesting site conspicuous. In areas where large numbers of birds congregate, the droppings may form thick layers, the so-called guano.

DRONGO: a member of the family Dicruridae. The twenty species of these passerines are found in the forests of the tropical parts of the Old World. They are iridescent black, usually with feather ornaments. Their feeding habit resembles that of *flycatchers*, as they live mainly on insects caught in the air. They are solitary in habits.

DROPPINGS: the mixture of urine and feces expelled from the *cloaca*. Before the droppings are expelled much of the liquid is re-

Ruffed grouse drumming

DRUMMING: the sound produced by the ruffed grouse with its rapid beating of the wings during display.

Yellowthroat removing dropping from young

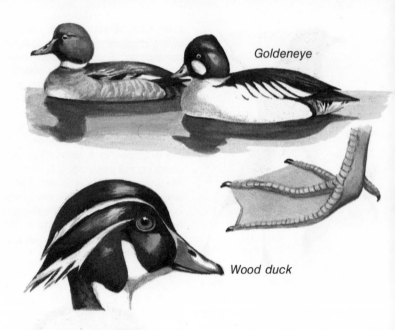

Goldeneye

Wood duck

DUCK: one of the smaller members of the family Anatidae (which includes ducks, *geese*, and *swans*). Ducks are divided into several subfamilies. The eight species of whistling ducks (Dendrocygninae) are confined to the tropics. They are long-legged ducks, usually frequenting marshes and swamps. Two species, the fulvous and black-bellied tree ducks, occur in North America and Antarctica. They are colorful and somewhat gooselike in appearance. The twelve species of perching ducks (Cairininae) are among the most brilliantly colored of ducks. It is to this subfamily that the wood duck of North America belongs. The single species of the torrent duck (Merganettinae) inhabits the swift-running streams of the high Andes. Of the forty-one species of dabbling ducks (Anatinae), no less than twelve occur in North America. This subfamily includes such common ducks as the mallards, black ducks, pintails, widgeons, and teals. Pochards, or bay ducks (Aythyinae), are rather plump diving ducks. Species like the canvasbacks, scaups, and ring-necked ducks belong to this group. The twenty species of sea ducks (Merginae) are all excellent swimmers and divers. The North American representatives include the eiders and scoters. There are nine species of stiff-tailed ducks (Oxyurinae) of which two, the ruddy and masked ducks, occur in North America. They are excellent divers.

DUCKLING: a young duck.

DUETTING: a term used for a special *song* in which a male and a female call simultaneously.

Canvasbacks

Black-bellied tree duck

Red-breasted merganser

DUSTING: behavior associated with the maintenance of the *feathrs* in which dust is pushed through the plumage. Many birds, especially those inhabiting deserts and other open, dry areas, perform dusting. Although the behavior in many respects resembles *bathing* and to some degree may serve the same purpose, the two acts are quite dissimilar. Certain species both bathe and dust, for instance the house sparrow. Dusting is usually performed in a small hollow and involves much wing flapping, fluffing of feathers, and shaking. The purpose of dusting is not well understood, but it may help the bird rid itself of various *ectoparasites*.

House sparrow dusting

E

EAGLE: any very large *hawk*. The term is rather ill-defined, but is mainly used in reference to any large *bird of prey* that is not clearly scavenging in its habits. In general, eagles are very large, broad-winged birds of prey that are aggressive and feed on mammals and birds. Their wingspread may

Bald eagle

reach eight feet. They vary from the enormously powerful harpy eagle to the much smaller but more agile hawk eagle. Although hardly any geographic area used to be without its species of eagle, relentless persecution has limited these spectacular birds of prey to remote mountainous regions or dense forests. In North America the golden eagle is a representative of the widespread genus of *Aquila*, and the bald eagle is a representative of a more restricted group of sea eagles. The bald eagle, the national bird of the United States, has suffered tremendously under the persecution of man, as well as from the widespread use of *insecticides,* limiting its fertility. It is now largely confined to a small population in Florida and a bigger one in Alaska.

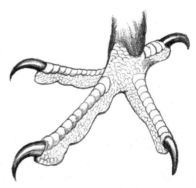

Golden eagle foot

EAR: the organ of hearing. In spite of its obvious lack of pinna, the protruding part of the outer ear so characteristic of mammalian ears, the avian ear greatly resembles ours. The external ear consists of a simple canal. The middle ear, similarly to that of the mammalian, consists of an air-filled space hrough which bony structures convey the vibrations of sound to the inner ear. The structure of the inner ear is identical to that of mammals, with a cochlea containing the nerve endings and the auditory nerve. The range of frequency of sound audible to birds is very similar to ours. Even within species using *echolocation* this is true. In some species the development of the ear shows special adaptations. The structure of the outer ear in owls differs between the right and the left side. This makes it possible

for the owl to locate the source of a sound with great accuracy. Experiments have shown that owls are capable of locating and catching their prey in total darkness on the basis of their specialized hearing apparatus.

ECHOLOCATION: the process used by some animals (bats in particular) to orient themselves. The animal emits sounds, the reflection of which orients the animal to the presence of obstacles or prey. Echolocation is used by two kinds of birds, *oilbirds* and

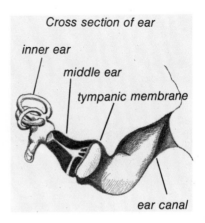

Cross section of ear

inner ear

middle ear

tympanic membrane

ear canal

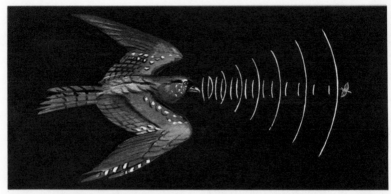

Oilbird locates its prey by the help of echolocation

certain types of *swifts*. Like bats, these birds nest in deep, dark caves where they have no visual clues for orientation and for navigation.

ECLIPSE: describing *plumage* that in certain birds, especially ducks, replaces the breeding plumage and is worn for only a short period of time. Even in male ducks this plumage is *cryptic*, resembling that of the female. It is present at the time the duck is flightless because of its molt.

ECOLOGY: the study of the interrelationship of an animal or a plant with its environment. In recent years it has become clear that ecological studies and considerations are of the utmost importance if we are to preserve many threatened species. Whereas *conservation* previously was aimed at particular species, it is now evident that not only the species but its entire environment must be taken into consideration if conservation efforts are to be successful.

ECTOPARASITE: a parasite living on the outside of the host's body. Ectoparasites are extremely common in birds. Several types occur, and among these a certain species may be limited in its parasitism to one or a few species of

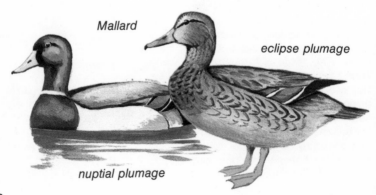

Mallard

eclipse plumage

nuptial plumage

Ectoparasites

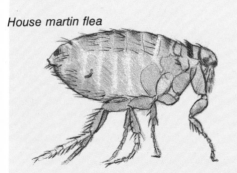
House martin flea

Headfeather louse

birds. All are flattened, an adaption to life among the feathers of their hosts. Most are flattened dorsoventrally, except for the fleas, which are flattened from side to side.

Fleas are relatively rare bloodsucking parasites. The eggs are laid in the host's nest. Feather lice have developed different species adapted to the different feather areas. They live largely on feathers and skin debris, but also on blood. Louse flies are large, flat insects, some with wings, some without. They are bloodsuckers. The pupae are found in birds' nests.

Ticks are commonly found on birds and some species exclusively parasitize birds. Ticks attach themselves to the host only for the time needed for sucking blood. Mites are very small parasites. The feather mites spend their entire life cycle on the bird, whereas red mites live in the nest, feeding on the birds at night.

Nests contain a large number of parasites. Ectoparasites may carry diseases, but unless infesting a bird very heavily, they cause little damage to the host.

EDIBLE NEST: a nest constructed by certain types of *swifts*, made by the bird's saliva and used in bird's-nest soup. Most of the species producing edible nests are colonial in their breeding habits and live in dark caves in the Far East.

EGG: the femals reproductive body (ovum) with its nutritive and protective layers. The egg is formed in the *reproductive system*. The egg yolk is the female reproductive cell, consisting of alternating layers of white and yellow yolk. On the surface of the yolk is the very small, white germinal spot where the *embryo* develops. The yolk is surrounded by the albumen, which again is covered by two membranes. These membranes are closely attached to the overlying eggshell except at the broad pole. Here an air space is present between the two membranes, only the outer of which is attached to the shell. The eggshell itself consists of a calcified layer of varying thickness. It protects the egg from damage. Air, but not fluids, is able to penetrate the shell through pores.

The size of eggs of different

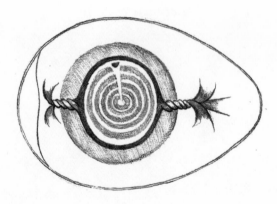

species of birds varies, with some exceptions, according to the size of the bird. The largest is the ostrich egg, which weighs 1,400 grams. The smallest is that of the hummingbird, weighing only .5 gram. The shape of the egg varies from species to species, but is consistent within each species. Some eggs are spherical, some oval, and some conical. The shape of the egg appears to a certain degree to be an adaptation to the number of eggs or to the degree of rolling at the nest site. The colors of eggs are also extremely varied. Eggs laid by ground-nesting birds usually have *cryptic* colors, often with many spots, making them difficult to see. Eggs of hole-nesting species are usually white.

The number of eggs laid by a certain species is called a *clutch*.

EGG TOOTH: the scalelike, sharp point on the upper part of the tip of the upper mandible found in the embryo and used for cutting through the eggshells when the young hatch. It is shed shortly after hatching.

1.	Puffin
2ab	Razorbill
3ab	Black guillemot
4.	Little auk
5ab	Black-tailed godwit
6.	Woodcock
7.	Honey buzzard
8.	Rock thrush
9.	Black woodpecker
10.	Green woodpecker
11.	Water rail
12.	Baillon's crake
13.	Little crake
14ab	Calandra lark
15ab	Water pipit
16abcd	Tree sparrow

From F. Graessner: Die Vogeleier, 1880

Oology, the study of eggs, reached its height in the late nineteenth century. Egg collecting, which today is outlawed in most countries, was a popular hobby in that period. Many beautifully illustrated books on eggs were published. This illustration is an example.

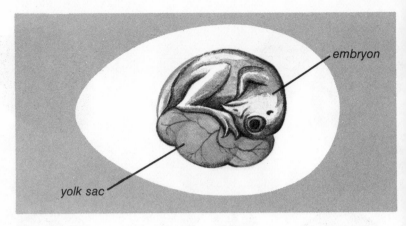

embryon

yolk sac

Embryo - 15 days

ELEPHANT BIRD: a member of the extinct family Aepyornithidae. Elephant birds were giant (up to 9 feet tall), ostrichlike birds found in Africa and Madagascar.

EMBRYO: an animal organism from the time of fertilization of the egg to hatching. At fertilization the sperm cell enters the still not fully developed egg and unites with the nucleus of the *egg* cell at the germinal disc. From this area the young develop, first while the egg is passing through the oviduct of the *reproductive system* and later during *incubation*. Through various stages of differentiation of the cells and foldings of different cell layers the embryo develops. In chickens the limbs are recognizable after about five days, the bill after about eight. By about the tenth day the embryo resembles a bird in its general characteristics. While developing, the embryo lives on the yolk and the albumen of the egg. Respiration takes place through the eggshell. Once the egg has hatched the bird is called a *young*.

EMU: a member of the family Dromiceiidae. There is only one living species, a large (up to 6 feet tall), ostrichlike bird found in open country in Australia. It is flightless. Emus are social in habits, and live on fruits and insects.

ENDOCRINE GLAND: a ductless gland that secretes hormones into the bloodstream.

Emu

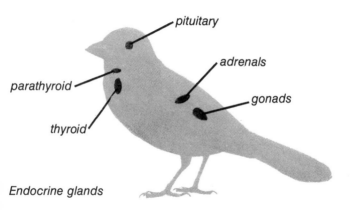

Endocrine glands

Endocrine glands include the pituitary, which secretes hormones affecting other endocrine glands, growth, and the urinary system; the thyroid gland, hormones from which affect the metabolism; and parathyroid glands, secreting hormones that have a profound effect on calcium and phosphate metabolism. The adrenal glands affect the heart rate, respiration, and several physiological processes. The pancreas affects sugar metabolism. The sex glands secrete hormones (either male or female) that affect the *reproductive system* as well as the behavior and secondary sexual characters.

ENDOPARASITE: a parasite living inside the host's body.

Endoparasites are common among birds. They fall into several groups, among which certain kinds might only affect certain species or groups of birds. Roundworms, such as ascarids, gizzard worms, gapeworms, and filariae, affect many different species of birds. The disease caused by the gapeworm and gizzard worm is often fatal, whereas other roundworm infes-

tations are easily tolerated by the host.

Tapeworms occur in many species affecting many different kinds of birds.

Flukes are likewise very common. They particularly affect waterfowl and shorebirds.

Many species of protozoa, single-celled animals, affect birds. Some cause malaria, others belong to the order Coccidia, mainly affecting the intestines, or to the genus *Trypanosoma,* where the infection in birds is much less severe than in man.

Fluke

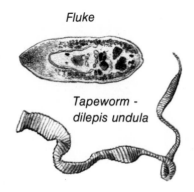

Tapeworm - dilepis undula

ETHOLOGY: the study of animal *behavior*.

EVOLUTION: the theory that various types of animals and plants have their origin in other pre-existing types, developing to their present form through modifications over generations. This theory, first brought forward convincingly by Charles Darwin in his book *the Origin of Species*, is now accepted by most biologists. The evolution of birds from reptiles to their present form is illustrated by such species as the *archaeopteryx* and other *fossil birds*.

EXCREMENT: in birds called *droppings*.

EXCRETORY SYSTEM: the organs involved in the elimination and excretion of waste materials. The most important of these are the kidneys and the urinary tract. As blood is filtered through the kidneys, waste materials in the form of excess salts and nitrogen-containing chemicals, uric acid in particular, are excreted as urine. The urine passes through the urinary tract to the *cloaca*, where it is expelled with the feces in the form of *droppings*. Besides the kidneys, the so-called salt glands, situated above the orbits, help in eliminating excess salt. These glands are highly developed in sea-birds and are able to excrete salt in very high concentrations.

EXTINCT BIRDS: species of birds that no longer exist. Usually the term is applied to birds that have become extinct within historic times, the term *fossil bird* being applied to those that disappeared in prehistoric times. More than seventy-five species have ceased to exist in historic times. These include such well-known birds as the dodo, great auk, passenger pigeon, Carolina parakeet, and labrador duck. Many species are threatened with extinction today, and great efforts are necessary to assure the *conservation* of such birds. The cause of extinction in most cases has been due to the influence of man, either directly through hunting (the dodo and the great auk), or through the introduction of predators like cats, dogs, and rats to areas where these animals were previously unknown and the birds had developed without specific adaptations to avoid these dangers. Flightless birds in particular have suffered greatly.

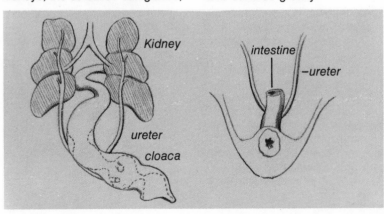

Kidney

ureter

cloaca

intestine

–ureter

Carolina parakeet

Heath hen

Great auk

Laysan Island rail

Riu kiu
kingfisher

Dodo

Huia

Passenger pigeon

Labrador duck

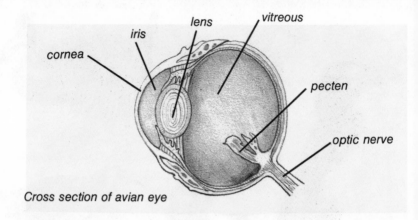

Cross section of avian eye

Labels: cornea, iris, lens, vitreous, pecten, optic nerve

EYE: the principal organ involved in vision. In birds the eye is highly developed and often very large. As in man, the eye consists of the cornea, the iris with its pupillary opening, the lens, the vitreous body, and the retina. In the retina the light stimulus is transformed into a nervous stimulus that travels via the optic nerve to the brain. The avian eye differs from the human by being much less spherical in its shape and by having an organ, the pecten, situated in front of the retina. The function of the pecten is unknown. The movements of the eyes are very limited, and birds look in different directions by moving the head. The eyes can be closed with eyelids, but besides this, birds possess a so-called nictitating membrane, a transparent membrane that can be pulled across the eye horizontally without shutting off all light. This aids in the protection of the cornea without impairing vision to any great extent. Most species of birds have monocular vision, but in species where exact depth perception is important, such as birds of prey, the eyes are situated farther forward, giving a large area of binocular vision. The colors most birds are able to perceive are smiliar to those perceived by man, although some species appear to have a somewhat poorer perception of blue light. Certain nocturnal species, like owls, which have a very sensitive light perception, may be partially colorblind.

Fairy bluebird

F

FALCON: a member of the family Falconidae. The family consists of the *caracaras*, the *forest falcons*, (both distributed in the New World only), and the cosmopolitan true falcons. True falcons vary in size from the six-inch-long Philippine falconet to the twenty-four-inch-long gyrfalcon. They have pointed wings and relatively long tails and are powerful flyers. Although variable in color, they are usually dark above, light below. They frequently catch their prey in the air with their feet. Many species have declined in numbers due to hunting and the wide use of *insecticides*. The North American representatives of the true falcons are the gyrfalcon, prairie falcon, peregrine falcon, aplomado falcon, pigeon hawk, and sparrow hawk, in descending order of size.

FALCONIFORMES: an order of *birds of prey* containing the families of *falcons*, *hawks*, *New World vultures*, *ospreys*, and *secretary birds*.

Peregrine falcon

Kestrel

Peregrine falcon

FALCONRY: the sport of hunting with *birds of prey*, *falcons* in particular. Falconry has been practiced for more than three thousand years in the Far East. It became popular in Europe during the Middle Ages, but since then has declined in popularity. Any bird of prey may be used, and training usually begins when the bird is very young.

FAMILY: in *taxonomy*, a group of genera (plural for *genus*) that closely resemble each other.

FEATHER: the light, horny structure that forms the *plumage*. Feathers are unique to birds and probably developed from the scales present in their reptilian ancestors. The typical feather consists of a shaft that is divided into the hollow basal part called the calamus and a solid, tapering proximal part, termed the rachis, which on each side supports a row of barbs that together form the vane of the feather. Branching from each barb are two sets of barbules supporting the barbicels, which on the proximal barbule are spoon-shaped, and on the distal, hooked. This arrangement of the barbicels in which the hooks of the distal barbicels fit into the proximal barbicels of the next barbule gives the feather its great strength and coherence. This description is of a contour feather, those feathers that form the outline of the bird, as well as the feathers of the wings and the tail.

Other kinds of feathers include semiplumes, which are usually shorter than contour feathers and lack the specialized barbicels giving the firmness of the vane of the contour feather. Semiplumes serve as insulation. Filoplumes are hairlike feathers, the function of which is unknown. Bristles are stiff hairlike feathers that occur around the mouth, nostrils, and eyes of many species of bird. The bristles about the mouth (rictal bristles) of such species as goatsuckers help in enlarging the effective gape by which insects are caught. Down consists of short feathers without a rachis. In the adult birds down is usually hidden underneath the contour feathers. A special kind of down is powder down, particularly common among herons. These feathers form a powder that covers the plumage. Many feathers have a so-called aftershaft, which is usually much smaller than the main feather and lacks the characteristic vane of the main feather. The aftershaft is of importance in insulation in many birds.

Remiges, feathers used in flight, are usually divided into the primaries, which are attached to the hand, and the secondaries, which are attached to the forearm. Other feathers of the wing are the wing coverts and the bastard wing, the

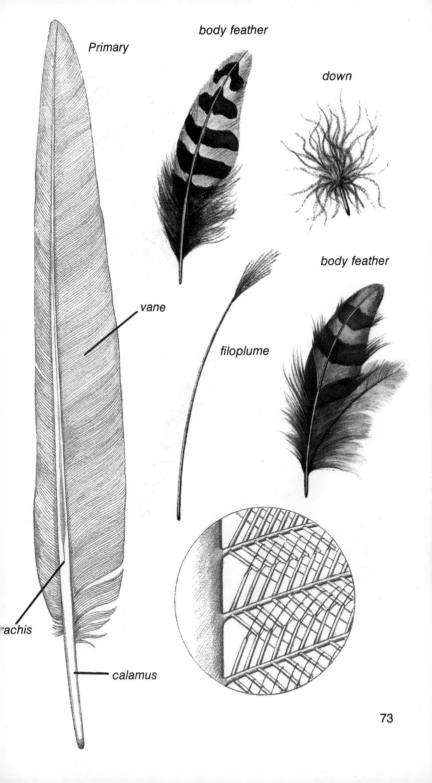

Primary

body feather

down

vane

filoplume

body feather

rachis

calamus

73

feathers attached to the thumb. The flight feathers of the tail are called rectrices. These are covered by the upper and under tail coverts. The feathers of the head, neck, and body do not grow evenly in most birds, but are restricted to certain areas, the so-called feather tracts (pterylae). These form a distinct pattern on the plucked bird. The number of contour feathers on an individual bird varies considerably, but is usually several thousand. The *colors* of the feathers are extremely variable. This variation in colors, as well as in some cases in the forms of feathers, is responsible for the various *plumages*. Plumages are changed and the feathers shed when the bird *molts*.

Contour feathers vary greatly in color and shape

Red-headed parrot-finch

Goldfinch

FINCH: one of many members of the families of *New World seed-eaters, goldfinches* and their allies, and waxbills. The term "finch" usually denotes a small, colorful, seed-eating bird.

FINFOOT: a member of the family Heliornithidae. There are three species of finfoots, or sungrebes as they are also called. They are long-necked, long-tailed, *anhinga*-like, medium-sized birds that frequent streams and lakes of tropical forests. They live on fish caught in the water, and are secretive in habits.

FIXED ACTION PATTERN: an inborn behavior pattern that is characterized by its lack of variation, its continuation without interruption, and its specific motivation. An example of such a fixed action pattern is egg-rolling behavior.

African finfoot

FLAMINGO: a member of the family Phoenicopteridae. The four species of flamingos are all very large, long-necked and long-legged wading birds with white or pink plumage. Flamingos are found in Europe, Africa, Asia, South America, and the Caribbean coast. They are social in their behavior. They feed on small animals and plant material, sieved from mud by their large, peculiar bill.

Greater flamingo

FLEDGE: to grow the plumage of true feathers of the young bird.

FLEDGLING: a young bird that has acquired the plumage necessary for flight, but is still dependent on the adults for food. The term is, however, ill-defined.

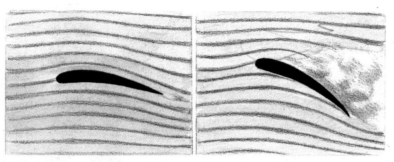

Patterns of air currents passing wings

FLIGHT: locomotion through the air by means of wings. The ability to fly is the outstanding characteristic of the class of birds. In *flightless birds* the ability has been lost as a secondary adaptation to their environment. Flight in birds is governed by the same aerodynamic principles that govern all flight. Lift is obtained by the streamlining of the wing. The convexity of the upper surface of the wing causes the air flowing past it to travel faster above the wing than below it. Through this phenomenon the pressure on the upper side of the wing is lower than the pressure on the underside. By tilting the wing upward, greater force is asserted on the underside; resulting in greater lift. The amount of tilt in relation to the direction of the wind flow is called the angle of attack. When the angle of attack is increased to such a degree that the airflow cannot follow the upper surface of the wing, turbulence is produced that causes the bird to stall.

Drag is the force of the air opposing the forward movement of the wing. The lift is increased as the wing area in the angle of attack increases, but an increase in speed increases the lift much more. Drag is also influenced by speed and wing area, but particularly by the angle of attack. Drag is to a large degree produced by the formation of air turbulence at the tip of the wings, called wingtip vortices. Birds which fly in V-formation utilize these vortices, since all birds, with the exception of the leader, get extra lift on the inner wing. The lift can be improved by the use of wing slots that increase the airflow over the wing by forcing the air to pass through a slot. The inner part of the wing serves as an airfoil, whereas the outer part of the wing, by its flapping action and flexibility, works almost as a propeller, giving the bird forward thrust. The direction of flight can be altered either by increasing the frequency of beating or by changing the angle of attack of one wing, thus making a difference in lift between the two sides. Twisting of the tail is also used as an aid in maneuvering.

The shape of the *wing* is adapted to the special types of flight performed by various birds. For instance, it is long and wide in soaring birds such as eagles and vultures.

77

Herring gull

Great blue heron

Brown pelican

Wandering albatross

Purple gallinule

Egyptian goose

78

Flamingo

Swallow-tailed kite

Tree swallow

Blue-cheeked bee-eater

Wood pigeon

Calliope hummingbird

Many of the anatomical and physiological characters of birds are especially adapted to flight. This is the case of *feathers*, the *skeleton, air sacs,* and the *vascular system*.

The speed with which birds can fly is variable, but usually lies between 15 and 60 miles per hour. The highest recorded speed is that of a peregrine falcon flying at 175 miles per hour.

FLIGHTLESS BIRD: a member of a species that has lost the ability to fly. Birds that have lost the power of flight are thought to have done so secondarily. This may either be as a positive adaption to their surroundings or as a more negative evolution in which the wings and the ability to fly have become of no value for the survival of the species. One whole superorder contains such families as the *ostriches*, *rheas*, *cassowaries*, *emus*, and *kiwis*, as well as the extinct *moas* and *elephant birds*. Members of the order of *penguins* have also lost the power to fly. In these the wings have become adapted for swimming and are very useful as such (positive adaption). Other species that have lost the power of flight include the dodo, the great auk, the flightless grebe, and the flightless cormorant, as well as several species of *rails*, such as the takahe of New Zealand. Two species of the South American steamer ducks have become flightless, although their wings are used to propel them forward over the surface of the water. Many flightless birds have, due to their vulnerability to predators, become extinct in modern times (see *extinct birds*).

Flightless birds

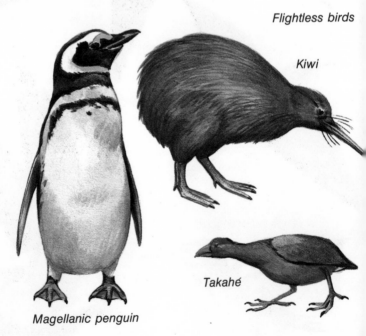

Kiwi

Takahé

Magellanic penguin

FLOCK: a group of birds that live, travel, or feed together. Many species form flocks for at least a part of the year. Often these flocks consist of members of the same species only, such as the tight flocks of starlings, but they may also consist of several different species, for instance, different warblers traveling together, different titmice feeding together, and different species of icterids roosting, traveling and feeding together. Within a flock a social structure of *dominance* often exists. Characteristic of many flocks is the remarkable synchronization of movements and behavior. Flocking is of survival value in regard to both obtaining food and avoiding predators.

FLOWER-PECKER: a member of the family Dicaeidae. The fifty-eight species of flower-peckers inhabit the tropical forests of Asia and Australia. Flower-peckers are small, short-tailed, and usually bright-colored *passerines* living on nectar and insects found in flowering trees and bushes.

Yellow-rumped flowerpecker

FLYCATCHER: a member of the family of *Old World flycatchers* or *tyrant flycatchers*.

Acorn woodpecker stores food in drilled out holes.

FOOD: the material furnishing nutrients. Birds utilize a large variety of the food items available in the world. Although some birds, like crows, are omnivorous, most are more particular in their choice of food. Some have become so specialized in their feeding habits that they are almost solely dependent on a single food item, as for instance, the Everglades kite, which feeds on snails of the genus *Pomacea* only. The shape of the *bill* usually reflects the feeding habits of a given bird. Some birds store food for later times. This is true of both the Canada jays and nutcrackers, as well as the acorn woodpecker. The food eaten by a given species in a certain area in most cases shows variation according to the season, mainly dependent on the availability of the preferred food. The food of the young is often different from that of the adult; thus many seed-eating birds feed insects to their young.

FOOT: the lower part of the *leg*.

FOREST FALCON: a member of the subfamily Herpetotherinae, which is part of the family of *falcons*. The five species of forest falcons inhabit the tropical forests of South America. They are medium-sized, long-tailed *birds of prey* that live on other birds. Their habits are poorly known.

Barred forest falcon

FORSTER, JOHANN REINHOLD (1729–1798): German naturalist who accompanied Cook on his second voyage around the world. A tern is named after him.

FOSSIL BIRD: the fossilized remains of a bird—a skeleton, or, more rarely, feathers.

Fossils of birds are relatively rare due to the fragile structure of their skeletons. However, at least 1,500 species have been found, about half of which are still living, the remainder having become extinct at various times. The oldest fossil bird is the *archaeopteryx*, which dates back about 150 million years. From the Cretaceous period, 63 to 135 million years ago, several fossils are known, among them the gull-like ichthyornis and a large, flightless diving bird, the hesperornis. From the Eocene epoch on, bird fossils become more common and include a larger variety of species.

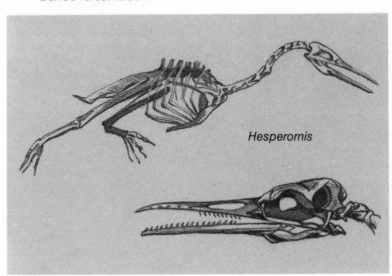

Hesperornis

Greater frigatebirds

FOWL: any of the members of the order Galliformes, which includes the *megapodes*, *chachalacas*, *grouse*, *pheasants*, *guinea fowls*, *turkeys*, and *hoatzins*. The term is often used especially for the domestic fowl, a member of the family of pheasants.

FRANKLIN, SIR JOHN (1786–1847): English navigator and explorer of arctic regions in particular. He disappeared exploring the Northwest Passage. A gull is named after him.

FRIGATE BIRD: a member of the family Fregatidae. The five species of frigate birds inhabit the tropical oceans of the world. They are large, long-tailed, and very long-winged seabirds that are gregarious in habits. They nest in colonies in trees, in bushes, or on rocks. They live on fish caught at the surface or stolen from other fishing birds. The magnificent frigate bird may be seen off the southernmost coasts of the United States, although it does not breed here.

FROGMOUTH: a member of the family Podargidae. The twelve species inhabit the forests of Asia and Australia. They are medium-sized, brown-speckled birds resembling nightjars, to which they are closely related. The mouth is very wide and the eyes large.

Tawny frogmouth

Woodpecker finch

Large cactus ground-fin[c]

Vegetarian tree-finc[h]

GALÁPAGOS FINCH: a member of the subfamily Geospizinae, which is part of the family of *New World seed-eaters* and related to *cardinals* and *buntings*. Galápagos finches are also called Darwin's finches. Thirteen species are found on the Galápagos Islands, and one on the Cocos Islands. These rather dull-colored finches are of interest because, through recent evolution, they have adapted to many different habitats. One of the species has even developed the unique habit of using a cactus spine to extract insects from holes and crevices. This is one of the few examples of the use of tools in birds.

GALLIFORMES: an order containing the families of *megapodes*, *curassows*, *grouse*, *pheasants*, *guinea fowls*, *turkeys*, and the *hoatzins*.

GALLINULE: any of a group of birds closely related to the *rails* and *coots*.

GAME BIRD: a bird that can be legally hunted. The term is primarily used for various species of *grouse*, *pheasants*, *ducks*, and *geese*, and also some species of shorebirds.

GANNET: a member of the family Sulidae, of which some species are also called boobies. The seven species of gannets and boobies are pelagic birds inhabiting the temperate and tropical oceans. They are large, usually black-and-white, long-winged birds with a strong, pointed bill. They live on fish they catch by diving headlong into the water. Gannets are social in their habits and nest colonially.

Gannet

84

GOATSUCKER: a member of the family Caprimulgidae. Goatsuckers are also called nightjars. The sixty-seven species of goatsuckers are found in all continents

Blue-grey gnatcatcher

Poorwill

GAVIIFORMES: an order containing the family of *loons*.

GENUS: a term used in *taxonomy* for a category including one species or a group of species that are closely related. The genus is given as the first part of the scientific name.

GIZZARD: a part of the *alimentary canal*.

GNATCATCHER: a member of the subfamily Polioptilinae. The eleven species of gnatcatchers and gnatwrens inhabit the temperate and tropical regions of the New World. They are closely related to the *Old World warblers* and are small, rather long-tailed birds usually found in bushes Gnatcatchers are usually blue-gray above, white below. They live on insects. Two species, the black-tailed and blue-gray gnatcatchers, inhabit the United States.

with the exception of Antarctica. They are medium-sized, long-winged, usually brownish birds that are nocturnal in their habits. They live on insects caught in flight. One species, the poorwill, is known to go into *hibernation*. The call of the goatsuckers is often characteristic and has given names to several of the North American representatives, such as the chuck-will's-widow, whippoorwill, and poorwill. Other North American representatives are the common and lesser nighthawks.

GOBBLING GROUND: the display ground used by the lesser prairie chicken of North America, where males gather to display for the females.

Emperor goose

Red-breasted goose

GOLDFINCH: a member of the family Carduelidae. There are 113 species of Goldfinches and the family is found on all continents excepting Australia and Antarctica. They are small, thick-billed, usually brightly colored, seed-eating birds that inhabit forests and scrublands. They are social in their habits. In North America the family is represented by such widespread species as the purple finch, house finch, and the rosy finches, redpolls and crossbills, as well as the American goldfinch.

GOOSE: a member of the sub-family Anserinae, which is part of the family Anatidae (*ducks*, geese, and *swans*). The fourteen species of geese inhabit the temperate and arctic areas of both the New and the Old World. They are large, long-necked birds, usually white, gray, or white, black, and brown. The greylag goose is the ancestor of the domestic goose, and the swan goose of the domestic Chinese goose. Geese are gregarious in their habits. The snow goose, Canada goose, and brant are common North American representatives of the subfamily.

GOULD, JOHN (1804–1881): English author and artist who wrote and illustrated books on birds from most parts of the world.

GREGARIOUS: tending to live in a flock.

GRIT: stones and pebbles eaten by birds to aid in digestion. Grit is particularly common in birds that eat vegetable matter, since the grit aids them in digestion by grinding the food particles. Grit is found in the gizzard, part of the *alimentary canal*.

GROSBEAK: a term used for some members of the subfamily Pyrrhuloxiinae (see *cardinal*).

GROUND ROLLER: a member of the subfamily Brachypteraciinae. The five species of ground rollers inhabit the forests of Madagascar. They are medium-sized, *roller*-like birds with duller colors and longer tails. They live mainly on insects caught on the ground.

GROUSE: a member of the family Tetraonidae. The eighteen species of grouse inhabit the forests, as well as open ground, of the temperate and arctic regions of both the New and the Old World. They are medium-sized to large, plump birds with short bills and legs. They vary in color from the almost solid black of the capercaillies to the pure white of the winter plumage of the ptarmigans. Most are, however, brown. They seek their food, which consists of various types of vegetable matter, on the ground. The courtship display is often social and elaborate. In North America the ptarmigans, prairie chickens, and ruffed and spruce grouse are examples of this family.

Capercaillie

Long tailed ground roller

Red grouse

GROWTH: increase in the size of the body. The growth of the *embryo* starts immediately after fertilization. After hatching, growth continues for a varying length of time. However, when the young have attained adult size, growth does not continue. Some species, for instance pelicans, attain a higher weight than the adult while they are still in the nest. This extra weight, however, is lost before the young become adult.

GRUIFORMES: an order consisting of the families of *bustards*, *collared hemipodes*, *cranes*, *finfoots*, *hemipodes*, *kagus*, *limpkins*, *rails*, *roatelos*, *seriemas*, *sun bitterns*, and *trumpeters*.

GUANO: the partially decomposed *droppings* found in large

Peruvian cormorant

quantities in seabird colonies and used as fertilizer. Guano is found in largest quantities on islands off the west coast of South America and southwest Africa.

Growth curve of house sparrow

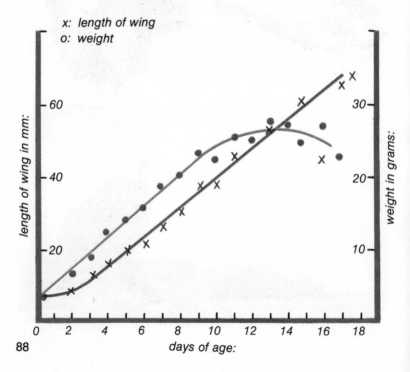

x: length of wing
o: weight

length of wing in mm:

weight in grams:

days of age:

10 days

7 days

15 days

juv. ad.

Growth of wheatear

8 days

1 day

Growth of herring gull

25 days

juv. ad.

89

Damara-crowned guinea fowl

Vulturine guinea fowl

GUINEA FOWL: a member of the family Numididae. The seven species of guinea fowls inhabit open areas in Africa. They are large turkeylike birds with strong legs and plumage that is mainly black with white markings. They are gregarious, ground-dwelling birds.

GULL: a member of the subfamily Larinae. Gulls and *terns* belong to the same family (Laridae). The forty-three species of gulls are distributed throughout the world with the exception of Antarctica. They are medium-sized to large, long-winged birds with strong, hooked bills. Most gulls are brown while immature, white with gray or black markings when adult. They are most common along seashores, but also inhabit inland waters. They are gregarious in habits and nest in colonies. Gulls are omnivorous.

Ring-billed gull

Laughing gull

H

Costa's hummingbird

HABITAT: the place where an animal or plant naturally lives and grows. Virtually all birds have a preference for a specific habitat, ranging from the open ocean to snow-covered mountaintops. This habitat preference may vary throughout the year. Scoters, for instance, prefer inland lakes for their breeding season, seashores in the winter. Destruction of a certain type of habitat, for instance a swamp or a marsh, will also destroy the birds adapted to that particular environment. Preservation of habitat, therefore, becomes of the utmost importance in the *conservation* of birds and it has become clear that large areas are needed.

HAMMERHEAD: the single member of the family Scopidae. The hammerhead is a large, long-billed, crested, heronlike bird with rather short legs. It is found in tropical Africa, where it frequents marshes and swamps, usually near trees. It lives on frogs and other aquatic animals.

HAMMOND, WILLIAM ALEXANDER (1828–1900): American neurologist and amateur ornithologist after whom the Hammond's flycatcher is named.

Hammerhead

HARCOURT, EDWARD WILLIAM VERNON (1825–1891): English politician after whom a petrel is named.

HAREM: a group of several females associated with one male. This relationship forms a type of *polygamy* that is not common among birds. An example is that of the male ostrich, which usually has several females in his harem. The females lay their eggs in the same nest.

HARLAN, RICHARD (1796–1843): American physician and friend of *J. J. Audubon*, who named a hawk after him,

Marsh harrier

HARRIER: a member of the subfamily Circinae, which is part of the family of *hawks* (Accipitridae). The seventeen species of harriers are long-winged and long-tailed, medium-sized hawks with owl-like faces. The males are usually brightly colored black, gray, or white, whereas females and immatures are brown. Harriers are found on all continents with the exception of Antarctica. They frequent open land and live mainly on rodents. The only North American representative of the subfamily is the marsh hawk.

HARRIS, EDWARD (1799–1863): American benefactor of *J. J. Audubon*, who named a hawk after him.

HATCHING: the emergence of the chick from the egg. The chick usually breaks through the egg with the help of its *egg tooth*. In most altricial birds the young is naked at the time of hatching, whereas in the precocial species it is covered with down. The order of hatching of the different eggs in a given *clutch* varies from species to species and may be synchronous. Usually, however, the egg laid first hatches first.

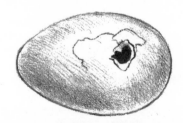

Two stages of hatching

HAWAIIAN HONEYCREEPER: a member of the family Drepanididae. The fourteen species of Hawaiian honeycreepers are limited in distribution to the Hawaiian Islands. They are small, rather drab-colored green, yellow, red, or black forest-dwelling birds. The members of the family vary tremendously in the shape of the bill, which can be long and decurved or short and conical. Besides the fourteen living species, eight have become extinct within historic times as the result of human interference with their natural habitat and the introduction of animals foreign to the Hawaiian Islands.

Honeycreepers

Kavai akialoa

Laysan finch

Liwi

HAWK: a member of the family Accipitridae. The family is by far the largest in the order of *birds of prey* (Falconiformes). The family is divided into several subfamilies: *accipiters*, *honey buzzards*, two subfamilies of *kites*, *harriers*, *Old World vultures,* and serpent eagles, and the subfamily of true hawks and *eagles*. True hawks are medium-sized, broad-winged usually rather short-tailed birds of prey. They are found on all continents with the exception of Ant-

Harris' hawk

Swainson's hawk

arctica. Most live on rodents that are caught either in open country or woodland. Hawks have a soaring flight. In North America the more common species of true hawks, or buteos, are the rough-legged, ferrunginous, red-tailed, red-shouldered, Swainson's, and broad-winged hawks.

HEART: a muscular pump situated in the chest cavity. The heart is part of the *vascular system*.

HEAT REGULATION: the mechanism that maintains a correct body temperature. Birds are warm-blooded animals and correct temperature is therefore relatively constant. The body temperature is maintained through the metabolism of nutrients and by heat dissipation. Although metabolism in some cases can become very low, as in *hibernation* and *torpidity*, it is mainly influenced by the activity of the bird. Subcutaneous fat, as well as the feathers,

Bustard quail (hemipode)

helps in conserving heat. Circulation of the legs is also adjustable, so heat can be conserved or dissipated to varying degrees. Heat is also dissipated by evaporation of water through the respiratory tract. Thus, in hot weather one can often observe birds panting rapidly. Other behavioral patterns have developed for the conservation of heat, the most spectacular of which is migration, by which birds avoid the extremely low temperatures of winter. *Roosting* in close proximity to other birds also helps conserve heat, as does the habit of many species of sleeping in tree cavities or rock crevices. The insulation of the nest is obviously of importance in conserving heat for the young. The temperature of birds is usually somewhat higher than that of man, around 106⁰ F.

HELMET SHRIKE: a member of the family Prionopidae. The nine species are limited in distribution to the woods of southern Africa. They are medium-sized, boldly colored passerines that live on insects.

HEMIPODE: a member of the family Turnicidae, also called button quail. The fifteen species of hemipodes are found in the southern part of Europe and Asia, as well as in Africa and Australia. They are small, chunky, quail-like birds, usually with brownish plumage. Hemipodes are found in semiopen and open country. The females are slightly larger and brighter colored than the males, and both incubate and care for the young.

HEN: a female bird; used specifically for the domestic fowl.

Great blue heron

HENSLOW, JOHN STEVENS (1796–1861): English botanist who was a strong supporter of Charles Darwin. A sparrow is named after him.

HERON: a member of the family Ardeidae, which also includes the *bitterns*. The sixty-three species of herons and bitterns are cosmopolitan in their distribution. Herons are medium-sized to large, long-necked, long-legged wading birds that frequent marshes, swamps, and seashores. There they catch fish and other aquatic animals with their long, pointed bills. Many species nest colonially in trees or bushes.

Hibernating poorwill

HIBERNATION: the act of spending the winter in a torpid state. Although hibernation is common among many other groups of animals, it is extremely rare in birds. It has only been described with certainty for one species, the poorwill, which is a goatsucker inhabiting the western part of North America. During hibernation the metabolic rate is much reduced and there is a prolonged period of *torpidity*.

HOATZIN: the single member of the family Opisthocomidae. The hoatzin is a large, pheasant-like, brown-crested bird inhabiting wooded river shores in northern South America. It is gregarious in habits and quite vocal. The young have claws on the wings that are used for climbing in bushes and trees.

HOMING PIGEON: a domestic pigeon used for carrying messages or racing. Homing pigeons are especially trained to return to their loft from increasing distances. They played a major role in communication before the time of telegraphy, but are now mainly used for racing.

HONEY BUZZARD: a member of the subfamily Perninae, part of the family of *hawks*. The thirteen species of honey buzzards are small- to medium-sized, long-winged birds of prey. Some, like the honey buzzard of Europe and Asia, are brown, broad-winged, soaring birds, whereas others, like the swallow-tailed kite of North America, are a beautiful black and white. The cuckoo falcons of Africa, Asia, and Australia are accipiters, like the honey buzzards, but have crests. Most of the honey buzzards are insectivorous.

Honey buzzard

HONEY-EATER: a member of the family Meliphagidae. The 172 species of honey-eaters inhabit Africa, Australia, New Zealand, and many of the Pacific islands. They are small- to medium-sized, slender-billed passerines, some of which are dull-colored, others very bright. They are quite gregarious in habits. Honey-eaters live mainly on nectar and insects. Some species are berry-eaters and may cause damage in orchards.

Greater honeyguide

HONEYGUIDE: a member of the family Indicatoridae. The eleven species of honeyguides are found in Africa and southern Asia. They are small, dull-colored forest dwellers. Honeyguides earned their name for their habit of leading animals and men to. bees' nests. When the nest is destroyed by the larger animal, the honeyguide will eat the wax. All honeyguides are parasitic in their breeding habits.

HOOPOE: the single member of the family Upupidae. Hoopoes are found in Africa, Asia, and Europe, usually in semiopen coun-

try. They are medium-sized, light-brown, black, and white birds with large, erectile crests. The bill is long and slender. Hoopoes live on insects and worms, and nest in tree cavities.

HOOTING: the calling of owls.

HORNBILL: a member of the family Bucerotidae. The forty-four species of hornbills are medium-sized to large, long-tailed birds with very large bills adorned with large casques. Whereas the bill and the casque are often brightly colored, the plumage is usually black, brown, and white. Hornbills are found in the forests in Africa and southern Asia. They are omnivorous, and nest in tree cavities. After laying the eggs the female walls herself in, covering most of the nest hole with clay or dung. She is fed by the male until the young are half-grown.

Hornbill

Hoopoe

Hummingbird nests

HOVERING: remaining suspended in a fixed position in the air by active wing movements. Many birds are able to hover, for instance kestrels, gulls, and hummingbirds.

HUMMINGBIRD: a member of the family Trochilidae. The 319 species of hummingbirds are restricted to the New World, and are particularly abundant in the tropical parts of South and Central America. Hummingbirds are small, and the family includes the smallest of all birds, the bee hummingbird, which is only 2½ inches long. Most hummingbirds are brilliantly colored green, blue, and red. The bill is long and slender but varies tremendously in length as well as in shape. Hummingbirds live on nectar obtained from flowers supplemented with some insect food. They are unique in their abilities in flying and can even fly backward. The most widespread North Ameri-

Swordbilled hummingbird

Streamer tail

Ruby-topaz hummingbird

Lawrence's warbler

Brewster's warbler

can species are the ruby-throated and rufous hummingbirds.

HYBRID: a cross between individuals of different species. Hybrids are rare among birds under natural conditions, but relatively common among birds kept in captivity. Within certain groups hybridization occurs with greater frequency than in others. This, for instance, is the case among many species of ducks. Several of these hybrids are fertile, contrary to common belief. In eastern North America two warblers, the golden-winged and the blue-winged, not uncommonly hybridize. Two forms of hybrids between these two species are known as Brewster's and Lawrence's warblers. Hybrids usually have obvious features inherited from both parents.

HYPOCOLIUS: the sole member of the family Hypocoliidae which inhabits semiopen country in the Near East. It is a small, rather long-tailed gray bird with social habits.

White ibis

IBIS: a member of the subfamily Threskiornithinae, which, together with the *spoonbills*, forms the family Plataleidae. The twenty-six species of ibises are medium-sized to large wading birds with long, decurved bills. They frequent fresh-water habitats in the warmer parts of Europe, Asia, Africa, and Australia, as well as in both North and South America. They vary in color from the plain red of the scarlet ibis of northern South America through the dark brown of the glossy ibis of cosmopolitan distribution to the pure white of several species, for instance, the sacred ibis of Africa. Ibises are gregarious in habits and nest colonially in bushes and trees or on the ground. They live mainly on various aquatic animals. The North American representatives of the subfamily are the glossy ibis, the very similar white-faced ibis, and the white ibis. The wood ibis belongs to the family of *storks*.

ICTERID: a member of the family Icteridae, also sometimes called American orioles. The eighty-eight species of icterids are found exclusively in the New World,

Scarlet ibis

White ibis

Redwing

Baltimore oriole

where they are very widespread. They are medium-sized, somewhat thrushlike passerines with a characteristic conical, pointed bill. A large number of the icterids are black, with or without iridescence in the plumage. Some, however, are very boldly patterned with black, yellow, and orange (orioles). A few are streaked brown, such as the meadowlarks and bobolinks. Their food consists of both animal and vegetable matter, and they inhabit a wide range of different habitats, from marshes to forests. Many icterids are gregarious in their habits and some are colonial nesters. Others, like the cowbirds, are nest parasites. Some of the more widespread and numerous of the North American representatives of this family are the meadowlarks, bobolinks, redwings, blackbirds, grackles, and Baltimore, Bullock's, and orchard orioles.

IMMATURE: a term applied to a young bird from the time it ceases being a *juvenile* until it becomes an *adult* and attains the stage of sexual maturity.

IMPRINTING: a *learning* pattern appearing in young birds, involving the recognition of its own species or a substitute. This learning process is confined to a very short period of the bird's life. An example of imprinting is the following response in young geese. When a gosling

Goslings imprinting on movable box

hatches it will follow the first rather large moving object that it sees. In nature this will be the mother bird, but under experimental conditions it may follow humans or even inanimate objects such as boxes that are moved around near it. The time period in which this is possible is quite short, but once established it becomes very stable. Thus the gosling may continue to regard humans as members of its species and respond sexually only to humans. Another example is the learning of the song pattern of a species in some birds like, for instance, the European chaffinch. In this case the song pattern is imprinted during the first year of the bird's life, at which point it becomes stable.

INCUBATION: the act of applying heat for the development of the embryo in the egg. Incubation in birds is done usually by one or both of the parent birds. In some cases, however, it may be done by members of other species (see *parasitic birds*). The *megapodes* do not incubate their own eggs, but take advantage of heat from the sun or from the fermentation of rotting plants or even from volcanic activity. The time of incubation is relatively stable in most species, but is to a certain degree dependent on the temperature applied to the egg. As this temperature in nature is rather constant, the incubation time is so, too. Albatrosses have the longest incubation times, which may reach as much as eighty days. Small passerines may have an incubation time that is as short as ten days, but is usually around two weeks. Incubation is, in most birds, facilitated by the presence of *brood patches*, which help in keeping the temperature relatively high. The incubating bird also turns the egg so that heat is applied to different parts at different times. After hatching, the parent bird will often *brood* the chick for a certain period.

INJURY FEIGNING: a type of *distraction display* in which a parent bird will distract a potential predator's attention from eggs or young by imitating the movements of an injured bird.

Sandgrouse injury feigning

INSECTICIDE: a toxic chemical used to combat insect pests. The recent increase in the use of synthetic insecticides has proved an extremely serious danger to wildlife. Two groups of insecticides are in wide use: the organophosphorous compounds, which are extremely toxic to the nervous systems of most animals but are decomposed rather rapidly, and the chlorinated hydrocarbons, which, although less toxic, are decomposed very slowly and which, when passing through a food chain of animals, tend to concentrate, thus particularly endangering the highest links of such chains. Insecticides may affect birds directly by causing their death when poisoned insects are ingested. They may, however, also have an indirect effect by causing infertility or congenital malformations. The chlorinated hydrocarbons, furthermore, appear to affect the thickness of the eggshell adversely, resulting in a large number of eggs being so thin-shelled that they are easily destroyed. Insecticides are thought to be responsible, at least in part, for the recent dramatic decline in such species as the bald eagle, brown pelican, and peregrine falcon. Restriction of the use of insecticides to areas where they are essential, as well as to types that are easily decomposed, appears to be the only way of controlling this extremely serious danger to us and our wildlife.

INSTINCT: an inborn capacity of an organism to give specific responses to environmental stimuli. The term is used to a decreasing degree as our knowledge of animal *behavior* and various aspects of *learning* increases.

INSTRUMENTAL SOUND: a sound made by nonvocal means. Instrumental sounds are produced by many birds. They include such things as the bull-clabbering com-

Common snipe's courtship dive - vibrating feathers

mon in storks, the whistling notes of the wings of many waterfowl, the drumming of the ruffed grouse, and the whirring sound produced by the outer tail feathers in several snipes during their aerial display.

INVASION: a term usually used for the rapid expansion of the range of a species into new areas. It is, however, often used to denote the *irruptions* characteristic of certain species.

IRIS: the opaque diaphragm perforated by the pupil and situated in front of the lens of the *eye*. The degree of contraction of the iris determines the size of the pupil.

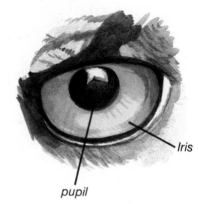

Iris

pupil

103

The iris may have different colors. Each species has its own characteristic color, dependent on sex and age. The color of the iris lends much to the visual impression one gets of a bird.

IRRUPTION: irregular migration in which certain species in certain years migrate to, and may even breed within, areas outside their normal range. Irruptions occur most often among species that are dependent on rather specialized food items. They occur when this food item, often after good crop years are followed by poor crop years, becomes scarce. The lack of the preferred food causes the bird dependent on it to invade other areas. Examples of such species are crossbills, which are dependent on spruce, cedar waxwings, which are dependent on berries, and snowy owls, which live primarily on lemmings.

ISOCHRONAL LINE: a line showing the boundary within which the same event occurs at the same time. In ornithology isochronal lines are particularly used to show the progression of *migration* of a certain species.

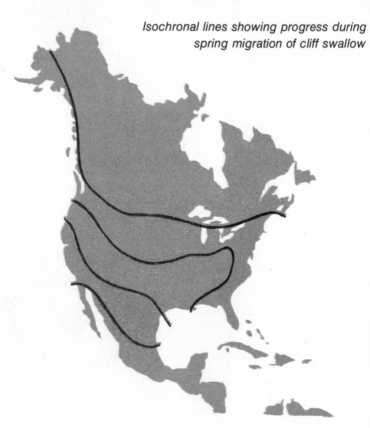

Isochronal lines showing progress during spring migration of cliff swallow

Blue jay

J

JACAMAR: a member of the family Galbulidae. The fifteen species of jacamars inhabit the tropical forests of Central America and northern South America. Jacamars are small- to medium-sized birds with long, pointed bills. Many have metallic, glittering plumage, giving them some resemblance to the hummingbirds, to which they are not related, however. Jacamars live on insects, which they catch in the air in flycatcher fashion. Most jacamars nest in burrows dug into banks or hillsides.

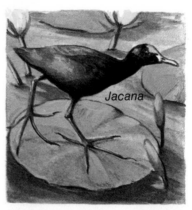
Jacana

Great jacamar

JACANA: a member of the family Jacanidae. The eight species of jacanas inhabit the tropical and subtropical parts of the entire world. Jacanas are medium-sized, brown, black, and white shorebirds with enormous feet. The very long toes enable the bird to walk on floating plants, which has earned it another of its names, "lilly-trotter." Jacanas inhabit marshes and swamps, as well as lake and river shores. There they seek their food, which consists of various sorts of aquatic animals and plants. One species reaches as far north as the southwesternmost part of the United States.

105

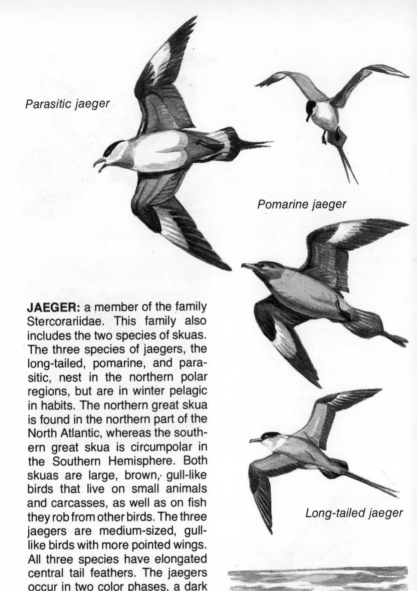

Parasitic jaeger

Pomarine jaeger

Long-tailed jaeger

JAEGER: a member of the family Stercorariidae. This family also includes the two species of skuas. The three species of jaegers, the long-tailed, pomarine, and parasitic, nest in the northern polar regions, but are in winter pelagic in habits. The northern great skua is found in the northern part of the North Atlantic, whereas the southern great skua is circumpolar in the Southern Hemisphere. Both skuas are large, brown, gull-like birds that live on small animals and carcasses, as well as on fish they rob from other birds. The three jaegers are medium-sized, gull-like birds with more pointed wings. All three species have elongated central tail feathers. The jaegers occur in two color phases, a dark brown one and a light phase in which the upper side is dark brown, the underside whitish. This *dimor-phism* is particularly common in the parasitic and pomarine jaegers. Like the two skuas, the jaegers are known for their *parasitic* habit of obtaining their food by robbing gulls and auks of their legitimately caught fish. However, in the breeding season they live to a large degree on rodents of the arctic tundra, and on lemmings in particular.

JAY: any of a group of smaller, more colorful members of the family of *crows*. The thirty-two species of jays are found in the Palearctic region and in North and South America. Jays are medium-sized birds with strong bills. Most are very colorful. They are forest dwellers that live on eggs and small birds, as well as on fruits and nuts. The largest concentration of species is found in the Americas. The more common and widespread species in North America are the blue, Steller's, scrub, pinyon, and gray jays.

JUVENILE: a *young* bird that is wearing its first plumage of true feathers. This stage in the development is preceded by the pullus and may be followed by an *immature* stage before the bird becomes sexually mature, or *adult*.

Scrub jay

Green jay

Steller's jay

Grey-headed kingfisher

K

KAGU: the sole member of the family Rhynochetidae, which is part of the order *Gruiformes*. The kagu inhabits the forests of New Caledonia and is becoming rare. It is a rather large, gray, heronlike bird with a characteristic crest and red bill and legs. It is mainly active at night, when it catches small animals found on the forest floor or in small ponds.

KINGFISHER: a member of the family Alcedinidae. The eighty-six species of kingfishers are small- to medium-sized, short-tailed, long-billed birds that are cosmo-politan in distribution, excepting the Antarctic. Kingfishers are mainly solitary in habits. Many live on fish, which they catch by diving headlong into the water either from a perch or from hovering flight. Others live on insects caught in the air or on smaller animals caught on the ground. They nest in burrows dug into banks or in tree holes. One of the largest kingfishers is the kookaburra, found in most of Australia. This species has a characteristic laughing call. The North American representatives of the kingfishers are the belted and green kingfishers.

Belted kingfisher

Pigmy kingfisher

White-tailed kite

Swallow-tailed kite

KITE: any of the members of the subfamily Elaninae (white-tailed kites) or the subfamily Milvinae (true kites), both part of the family of *hawks*. The white-tailed kites are small birds of prey found mainly in open country. Members of this subfamily are found in the Americas, southern Europe, and Asia, as well as in Africa and Australia. They are usually colored black, gray, and white. The North American members of this subfamily are the white-tailed and Mississippi kites. The true kites are found mainly in the Old World, but are represented in North America by the Everglades kite. They are medium-sized, rather broad-winged, mainly brownish or black birds of prey, many of which have forked tails. One species, the black kite, is primarily a scavenger, and is often seen by the hundreds near towns and villages in the warmer parts of the Old World.

KIWI: a member of the family Apterygidae. The three species of kiwis are found only in New Zealand, where they inhabit forests and swamps. Kiwis are medium-sized, dark-brown, flightless birds with long bills used for probing into the ground for worms and insects. They nest in burrows. The egg of the kiwi is very large in proportion to the bird. The egg of an eight-pound bird may weigh one pound.

Kiwi

Lammergeyer

LAPPET: an unfeathered fold or flap of skin situated near the bill. Lappets are often brightly colored and appear to serve an ornamental purpose. Lappets are found in such families as the pheasants and the starlings.

LARK: a member of the family Alaudidae. The seventy-eight species of larks· are distributed throughout the world, with the exception of most of South America and Antarctica. They are small- to medium-sized passerines with long, pointed wings. The plumage is usually brown or gray with brown· or black spots or markings. Larks are terrestrial in habits and, outside the breeding season, usually occur in flocks. Their songs are quite varied and musical and are often given in flight. They live on insects and seeds found on the ground. They inhabit open grasslands and fields, as well as deserts. The sole North American representative of the family is the horned lark, which has two small crests.

LAWRENCE, GEORGE NEW-BOLD (1806–1895): American pharmacist and ornithologist who was particularly interested in birds of the tropical Americas. A goldfinch is named after him.

LAY: to deposit an *egg*. After the egg has been formed and covered with its shell in the *reproductive system*, it is expelled through the vagina and the *cloaca*. In most species the egg is laid with the pointed pole first, but in others the blunt pole is first. The time it takes for the bird to lay the egg varies from species to species. The fastest egg layers are the *par-*

Horned lark

asitic birds, such as the cuckoos and cowbirds, which may take only seconds. Larger birds, like geese and swans, may have to labor for several hours.

Egg laying starts when the female is sexually mature. In domestic chickens this happens after about six months, whereas in most wild birds it takes one year. Larger species may take several years to become sexually mature, and some albatrosses may not start laying until eight years of age. Egg laying in wild birds is restricted to a specific *breeding season*. Several domestic birds, however, do not have a specific breeding season and may lay all year round. Egg laying is often restricted to a particular time of day, most often early in the morning. The number of eggs laid in a *clutch* varies from species to species, but is usually quite constant within a given species. In some birds the number can be artificially varied by removing eggs during the egg laying. Such birds will then lay additional eggs to replace those removed. These birds are called indeterminate layers. In others, called determinate layers, such manipulations have no influence.

LEACH, WILLIAM ELFORD (1790–1836): English naturalist of great renown. A petrel is named after him.

LEAFBIRD: a member of the family Irenidae. The fourteen species inhabit the forests of Oriental regions. They are rather small passerines with slightly decurved bills and brightly colored, fluffy plumage. Most are social in habits. They live on fruits, berries, and insects, which they find in treetops.

LEARNING: the development of adaptations in behavior as the result of experience.

Imprinting, through which the young bird learns to recognize its own species, is a type of learning limited to a short period of time. Other kinds of learning include habituation, through which the bird learns to recognize phenomena as being harmless or unrewarding. An example of habituation is the change in response to a human being as a bird is being tamed. The conditioning through which the bird learns to respond specifically to a given stimulus has been of great importance in the investigation of the capacities of the various sense organs. Learning by trial and error obviously plays a major role in the adaptation of a bird to its surroundings. During this process the bird will, for instance, gain knowledge about the appropriate food items. Insight learning, as we know it from humans and higher mammals, has been demonstrated in only a few instances among birds. An example is the ability of some species to count.

Golden-fronted leafbird

LE CONTE, JOHN (1818–1891):
American physician and amateur naturalist after whom a sparrow is named.

LE CONTE, JOHN LAWRENCE (1825–1883): American entomologist after whom a thrasher is named. He was a cousin of John Le Conte.

LEG: one of the two hind limbs. Although containing the same elements as a human leg, the bird's leg differs in proportions. The thigh is shorter and well hidden in the contour feathers. Some of the foot bones have become fused with the tibia to form the tibiotarsus, which stretches from the knee to the ankle. Other foot bones have fused with each other (both metatarsal and tarsal bones) to form the tarsometatarsus, which stretches from the ankle to the toe and corresponds to our instep. The term "tarsus" is used for both bone and covering skin, feathers or scales. The toes are usually four in number, but may be three or even two, as in the ostrich. The shape of the leg, and particularly the foot, varies tremendously from species to species, but is usually adapted to either grasphig, walking, or swimming. In most birds the toes are covered with scales, but in some, like the ptarmigans, they are covered with feathers. Three main functional types of feet can be recognized: a perching type, which has a good grasp, a type for walking and wading with long, straight toes, and a type for swimming, in which the toes may be webbed or lobed.

The tendons stretching to the toes are arranged in such a fashion that the strength of the grasp increases as the leg is bent. The blood vessels supplying the feet are equipped with shunting mechanisms that can be used in *heat regulation*.

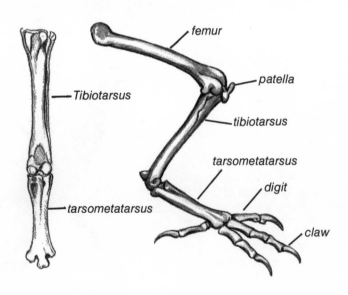

Tibiotarsus

tarsometatarsus

femur

patella

tibiotarsus

tarsometatarsus

digit

claw

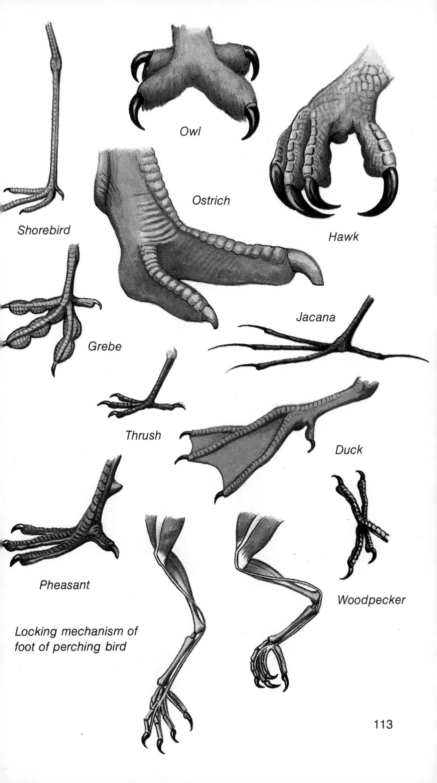

Owl

Ostrich

Shorebird

Hawk

Jacana

Grebe

Thrush

Duck

Pheasant

Woodpecker

Locking mechanism of
foot of perching bird

113

Lek display by black grouse

LEK: a type of social *display* performed by several male birds on special display grounds. Lek displays are among the most spectacular phenomena in the world of birds. The display usually involves elaborate movements and positions by which highly colored parts are displayed. This is often associated with the production of loud noises and, occasionally, with fights between cocks. Females are attracted to the arenas and will usually mate with the dominant male. Lek display is performed by a large number of different species of birds, but is particularly common among grouse, pheasants, and cranes, and is also found in some species of shorebirds and passerines. The arenas are often used year after year and may go under such names as *booming grounds* and *gobbling grounds*.

LEWIS, MERIWETHER (1774–1809): American officer and explorer who together with William Clark traveled in the northwestern part of the United States. He was murdered, or committed suicide, on a journey to Washington, D.C. A woodpecker is named after him.

LICHTENSTEIN, A. A. H. (1753–1816): German naturalist and theologist after whom an oriole is named.

LIMPKIN: the sole member of the family Aramidae. The limpkin is a rather large, long-legged, long-necked, and long-billed bird related to the *cranes*. It has a brown plumage spotted with white. The limpkin inhabits swamps and marshes of the southeastern United States, Central America, and northern South America. It is solitary and rather secretive in its habits. Its food consists mainly of snails. The limpkin has a great variety of wailing and screaming calls that are often given at night.

Limpkin

Red-throated loon

LINNAEUS, CAROLUS (1707–1778): Swedish botanist and the founder of modern systematics in both botany and zoology. His original name was Carl von Linné.

LOCOMOTION: the act of moving from place to place. Several methods of locomotion are practiced by birds. Many are, of course, experts in *flight*. Others excel in swimming, and almost all can walk or hop. Some species, like the woodpeckers, are especially adapted for climbing up tree trunks. Many parrots climb through tree-tops with the help of their bill as well as their feet.

LONGEVITY: length of life. The longevity of different birds varies greatly. As in most animals, *mortality* is highest during the first year of life, after which it usually decreases markedly to a constant rate. The actual life-span of most birds is, therefore, far shorter than the potential life-span. Birds in captivity have reached very high ages (an eagle owl has been recorded as reaching the age of sixty-eight), but such ages can probably not be attained in the wild. Among the oldest ages attained by free-living birds are those found among gulls, shorebirds, and birds of prey, which may attain an age of more than thirty years. Most smaller birds, however, live no more than five to eight years.

LOON: a member of the family Gaviidae, also called diver. The four species of loons are found in the northern part of the Northern Hemisphere. They breed on smaller fresh-water lakes or rivers but spend the winter along sea-shores or in large lakes. Loons are rather large diving birds with pointed bills. In winter they are dark gray above, white below. In summer they have characteristic black-and-white patterns on the head, neck, and back. They are quite solitary in habits. Loons live on fish caught under water. All four species, the common, white-billed, arctic, and red-throated loons, nest in North America.

LORE: the area between the upper part of the bill and the eye.

LYREBIRD: a member of the family Menuridae. The two species of lyrebirds are found in the forests of Australia. They are rather large, pheasantlike passerines. Lyrebirds are brown in color, and the males are adorned with an enormous lyre-shaped tail that during the breeding season is often beautifully displayed. Lyrebirds are solitary in habits. They live on insects and other small animals found on the forest floor.

Lyrebird

M

Golden-headed
manakin

MACAW: the name for some members of the family of *parrots*. They are the largest and most colorful of the family and are found in the New World from Mexico south to Argentina.

MACGILLIVRAY, WILLIAM (1796–1852): a Scottish naturalist who was associated with J. J. Audubon and after whom Audubon named a warbler. He is also the auther of *A History of British Birds*, a major ornithological work of its time.

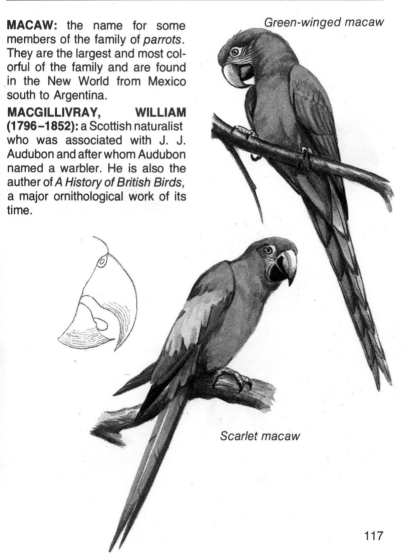

Green-winged macaw

Scarlet macaw

MAGPIE: name used for certain species of the family of *crows*. Magpies are medium-sized, usually long-tailed and very colorful birds. Several different species occur in Asia. The most widespread is the blackbilled magpie which is common through most of the Palearctic region as well as in the western parts of North America. The other North American representative is the yellowbilled magpie.

MAGPIE-LARK: any of the members of the family Grallinidae, also known as mudnest builders. The four species of this family are limited in distribution to Australia and New Guinea where they inhabit open and semiopen country usually near water. They are medium-sized to large gray, black and white birds. Outside the breeding season they are often gregarious. They build nests of mud.

MALAR: the side of the throat just below the mandible.

MANAKIN: member of the family Pipridae. The fifty-nine species inhabit the forests of Central and South America. They are small, short-winged and short-tailed passerines in which the males often have boldly contrasting colors. The females are much duller colored. They are mainly fruit eaters. They are polygamous in their nesting habits.

Magpie-lark

Magpie

Chestnut mannikin

Red-backed mannikin

MANNIKIN: name used for several species of the family of *waxbills*.

MASSENA, ANNA de BELLE (1806–1896): the wife of Duc de *Rivoli* who was a close friend of Audubon. A hummingbird is named after her.

MCCOWN, JOHN PORTER (1817–1879): American officer and naturalist after whom a longspur is named.

MCKAY, CHARLES LESLIE (?–1883): American officer and naturalist after whom a bunting is named. He drowned when his boat capsized.

MEASUREMENT: Several standard measurements are used in birds which are of particular importance in *taxonomy*. The total length is the distance from the tip of the bill to the longest tail feather with the bird stretched out. The wingspan is the distance between the wingtips when the wings are fully extended. The wing length is the distance from the bend of the folded wing to the tip of the longest flight feather. The length of the tail is the distance from the tip of the

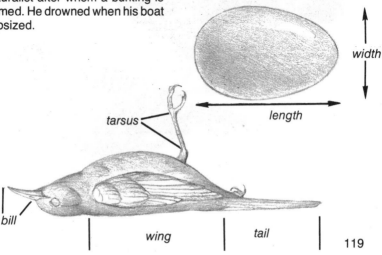

width

length

tarsus

bill

wing

tail

119

longest tail feather to the point on the skin where the central tail feathers emerge. The bill length is measured from the tip of the upper mandible to the base of the feathers on the head or to the cere. The length of the tarsus is measured from the heel to the base of the upper side of the middle toe.

Eggs are measured in regard to length and breadth.

Whereas total length and wingspan might be expressed in inches, most other measurements are given according to the metric system.

MEGAPODE: a member of the family Megapodiidae. The ten species of megapodes are ground-dwelling, rather long-legged birds closely related to other members of the order Galliformes. In distribution they range from Australia northeastward to the Philippines.

The family includes such species as brush turkeys, mallee fowl and the Australian jungle fowl. The megapodes are medium-sized to large brownish birds, most with rather long tails. Most are forest dwellers, but one, the mallee fowl, is found in dry scrubland. The nesting habits of megapodes are unique and have earned the group such alternative names as mound builders and incubator birds. In none of the species does the parent bird incubate the eggs itself. In some the eggs are merely buried in some sand which is exposed to the sun which provides the heat necessary for the development of the fetus. Other species depend on volcanic activity to supply the heat by burying their eggs in ashes found near such active volcanos. Most, however, construct large mounds in

Brush turkey

Mallee fowl

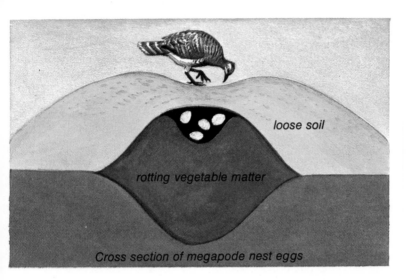

loose soil

rotting vegetable matter

Cross section of megapode nest eggs

the center of which the eggs are buried. These mounds consist of vegetable matter covered with loose soil. The fermenting of the vegetable material produces the heat necessary for the incubation. During the time of incubation the mound is attended by the male which, by adding or removing cover and plant material, keeps the temperature within necessary limits. When the young hatch they are highly developed and able to fly. After digging their way out of the mound they care for themselves without parental guidance.

MELANISM: a condition caused by an excess of dark pigment in the plumage. Various degrees of melanism occur causing the plumage of the individual to appear darker than the normal.

MERGANSER: a term used for certain members of the subfamily of sea *ducks*. Mergansers have rather long, narrow bills with serrated edges. They are excellant divers. The American, the red-breasted and the hooded mergansers are North American representatives of the group.

METABOLISM: refers to the chemical changes occurring in an organism after the nutrients have been absorbed from the *alimentary canal*. Through enzymatic processes and in combination with oxygen, fats and carbohydrates are broken down into carbon dioxide, and water and heat are released. Protein is broken down in a somewhat similar fashion but much of its nitrogen content is used in the buildup of other tissue cells, or is excreted as uric acid. The metabolic processes are of great importance in *heat regulation* as well as in *growth* of tissues.

MIDDENDORF, ALEXANDER T. (1815–1894): a Russian explorer and zoologist of German descent who was among the most outstanding naturalists of his time. A warbler is named after him.

MIGRATION: the periodical movement from one region to another for the purpose of feeding or breeding. Although many animals migrate the most spectacular example of this phenomenon is the migration of birds.

The migration of birds has been observed since ancient times. It is alluded to in the Bible. The ancient Greeks were well aware of the migration of birds as attested to by Aristotle's description in *History of Animals*, as well as by many quotes from classical authors. The concept that birds disappeared for a certain period of time because they migrated and not because of *hibernation* did not, however, win universal acceptance until the 19th century.

Aristotle wrote on the migrating flocks of cranes

The migration of birds is studied in several different ways. The observation of the presence or absence of a given species at a certain place and time is of obvious importance. The systematic collection of such observations helps

European crane

Migration of golden plovers in America

Nocturnal migration can be watched against the moon or on radar.

define the breeding areas as well as the wintering grounds. The observation of birds flying past a certain area involved in actual migration is of help in determining the direction and routes followed by the various species. At night this method is obviously very difficult. However, it is possible by watching the moon through a telescope to ascertain how a sample of night migrants move. This method is called moon watching and has been particularly used in the United States. Much more information, however, has been gained by the use of radar. Radar is now so refined it is able to track even small birds over long distances and has aided tremendously in our understanding of migration and *orientation*. The shortcoming of this method is its inability to distinguish species.

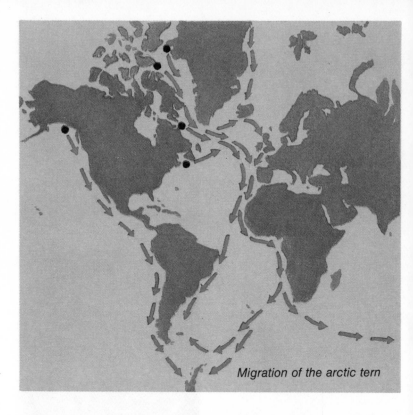

Migration of the arctic tern

Since the introduction of bird *banding* in 1899, this method of studying migration has become the most important. The banding of young on the breeding grounds and the subsequent recovery in another area has given information about wintering areas, migratory routes, and times, as well as about speed of progress. The banding of birds at special observatories set up along the major routes and concentration points of migratory birds has been particularly important in the study of details in migratory patterns.

Although migration is a widespread phenomenon in the avian world, it is far from universal. In the tropics in particular where the climate throughout the year might vary little, many, if not most, species do not migrate. In the temperate zones such species as the great tit in Eurasia and the chickadees in North America are species enduring the inhospitable winters in the general area of their breeding grounds. Other species are partial migrants, meaning that part of the population of a certain species migrates, whereas another part does not. An example of this is the fox sparrow of western North America. Whereas the northernmost breeding population migrates hundreds of miles in fall, more southern breeders remain on their breeding grounds throughout the year.

True migrants may cover thousands of miles each fall and spring. The Arctic tern, nesting in the Arctic, thus traverses the equator to spend the northern winter on the seas surrounding the Antarctic continent. It is the animal which experiences the most sunlight, enjoying the midnight sun of both circumpolar regions. Wilson's petrel, a small seabird nesting on islands in the southern Antarctic, spends its winter (the northern summers) in northern oceans, although not covering quite the distance of the Arctic tern. The short-tailed shearwater is a medium-sized seabird which nests off southern Australia. Its travels take

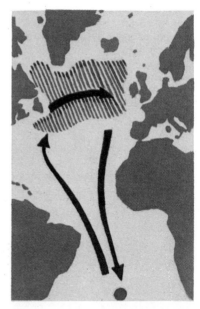

Migration of the greater shearwater

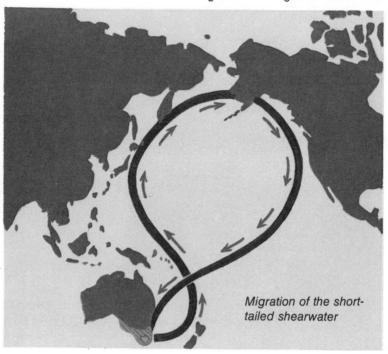

Migration of the short-tailed shearwater

125

it in a circular route across the Pacific all the way to the waters off North America.

But not only seabirds travel far: the white stork of Europe thus spends its winters in South Africa; bobolinks of North America travel to the South American pampas; bronze cuckoos from southern Australia and New Zealand travel to New Guinea and adjacent islands in March and April, etc.

Although most birds migrate in a north-south direction, this is not universally true. The direction is greatly influenced by the local climate and geography. In North America many birds fly in a south-easterly direction in fall, whereas most European migrants take a southwesterly course in the fall season.

The migration may be vertical where species nesting in the high mountains seek refuge in the valleys for the winter.

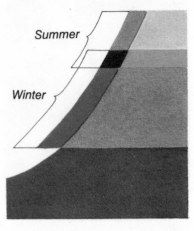

Summer

Winter

Schematic representation of vertical migration in alpine birds

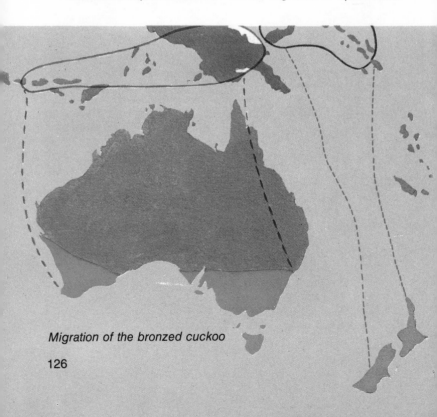

Migration of the bronzed cuckoo

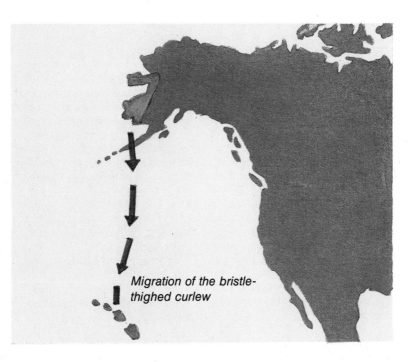

Migration of the bristle-thighed curlew

The speed with which migration is performed varies greatly from species to species. For many kinds of birds the actual flight speed is known. It varies from about 15 mph in small passerines to 60 mph in swift-flying ducks. Although some species may cover most of the distance from breeding to wintering grounds in one uninterrupted flight, this is not true of most migrants which usually interrupt their migratory flight for periods during which they rest and feed. Examples of the long-distance migrants which travel uninterrupted are the golden plovers nesting in Alaska and the bristle-thighed curlew, which leave the coast of Alaska not to land until they have reached Hawaii, 2,000 miles further south. The journey has been calculated to require at least 35 hours of uninterrupted flight and one quarter of a million wingbeats.

The height at which migrating birds fly varies tremendously. Many seabirds travel but a few feet above the waves, whereas landbirds may fly as high as 15,000 feet above the ground. When passing over mountains the migrating birds might be forced to fly very high above sea level. The record in this respect is held by a flock of bar-headed geese which flew at an elevation of almost 30,000 feet when crossing the Himalayan mountains.

Migrations are strongly influenced by weather conditions. Rain often stops migration altogether as do extremely strong winds. Winds of moderate strength may blow migrating birds off their course and sometimes may cause concentration in certain areas such as along coastlines or on islands where landbirds try to avoid the perils of an overseas journey. The combination of weather and geographical features such as mountains and coastlines may also cause the birds to concentrate along certain routes. This is especially true of large-winged soaring birds such as hawks and eagles. These species may be observed in large numbers as they follow the Appalachian mountains of eastern North America southward in fall, or at the Bosphorus as they pass from Europe to Asia. However, most birds migrate over broad fronts or follow rather wide flyways. An example of this latter mode are the flyways followed by North American waterfowl.

Some birds migrate only irregularly, causing *irruption*.

Some waterfowl migrate to certain areas prior to their molt, known as molt migration.

The stimulus which sets off migration is variable. For many species it appears that the change in length of day is the determining factor, whereas in others it seems to be such factors as rainfall or changes in temperature. However, the internal stimulus is more important. The physiology of migration is closely interrelated with the breeding cycle and both are hormonally determined.

The manner in which the migratory bird finds its way, often over thousands of trackless miles, is described under the heading of *orientation*.

Major migratory routes (flyways) of North America

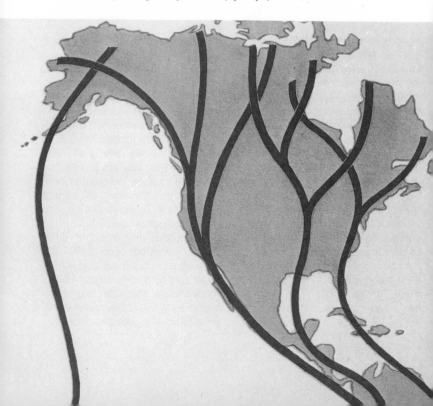

The cuckoo resembles the European sparrowhawk

MIMICRY: The practice among birds of imitating the songs of other birds or other sounds is quite common. Certain species are exceptionally skilled in this respect. This is particularly true of such species as mockingbirds, bowerbirds and starlings, but many other species are able to incorporate parts of songs of others in their own. Even more striking is the imitation of human speech by certain parrots and mynahs kept in captivity. When these birds are deprived of social contact with others of their species, they quite easily pick up various words and even sentences. However, they do not appreciate the content of the sentence they mimic.

Mimicry in the form of advantageous resemblance to other birds in plumage is rare among birds. However, the striking resemblance between certain cuckoos and some birds of prey is an example. Another is the resemblance of the young of certain parasitic cuckoos to the young of their host.

MIMINE THRUSH: a member of the family Mimidae. The thirty-one species of mimine thrushes are known as catbirds, mockingbirds and thrashers. In distribution they are limited to the New World where they inhabit brushland, gardens and open forests. They are medium-sized to rather large passerines which in general outline resemble the thrushes. Some are quite uniformly colored, whereas others have more striking patterns in the form of breast spots or wing patches. The general colors vary from brown through gray to black. The mimine thrushes are solitary in their habits and most are non-migratory. They are excellent singers and several are very good mimics, the mockingbird in particular.

Brown thrasher

Catbird

Moa

feathers are also shed gradually. In this way the ability to fly is not impaired. Some birds, however, (waterfowl, rails, auks, and loons) lose all their flying feathers simultaneously but their aquatic lifestyle helps them elude enemies although for a period they are rendered flightless.

Although very variable from species to species, the sequence

Molting of scarlet tanager

fall

molting

spring

MOA: a member of the order Dinornithiformes which is extinct. Remains of moas have only been found in New Zealand. They were very large (up to 10 feet high) ostrichlike birds.

MOBBING: a common reaction among birds to a perched hawk or owl. By their constant fluttering and warning calls other birds in the area are alerted to the presence of the predator, and the predator itself might be distracted enough not to discover the young in the neighborhood.

MOCKINGBIRD: a name used for about half the members of the family of *mimine thrushes*.

MOLT: the periodic loss and subsequent renewal in birds of the *plumage*. This process takes place in an orderly fashion except in penguins where the feathers seem to be shed in a totally disorderly pattern. The molt is symmetrical and usually starts with a shedding of the inner primaries, progressing outward on the wing as the first ones are being replaced. Secondaries and tail feathers are shed in a similar fashion. The body of molts resulting in the adult plumage usually follows a certain pattern: the natal downs are lost at the post-natal molt. The juvenile plumage is shed during the post-juvenile molt and replaced by the first winter plumage. In the following spring this is shed in the first pre-nuptial molt, being replaced by the first nuptial plumage. After breeding the first post-nuptial molt occurs, giving the bird its second winter plumage. In most small birds the first nuptial plumage is that of an adult and only two different plumages are recognized from this point on, a winter and a summer plumage. These two adult plumages are attained through two annual molts, the pre-nuptial and the post-nuptial.

Although most birds molt but twice a year, some, such as the ptarmigans and some shorebirds, may molt three or four times.

The time of molting is closely correlated with the *breeding* cycle and with *migration*. Thus most birds complete their post-nuptial molt prior to migrating. The pre-nuptial molt is clearly preparatory to breeding activity. Like the breeding cycle and migration, the molt is hormonally determined.

MOON WATCHING: a method of studying *migration* at night.

MORPH: denotes any one of the different forms in species where *dimorphism* or polymorphism exist.

MORTALITY: the rate of death. Among birds the mortality is by far the highest in young birds. However, in all birds studied the mortality rate of the adult is constant. Mortality rates vary tremendously from species to species and are highest in small birds but extremely low in, for example, albatrosses and large birds of prey. The mortality rate is obviously of great importance in the study of bird populations.

MOTMOT: a member of the family Memotidae. The eight species of motmots inhabit central and northern South America here they are found in rain forests. They are medium-sized, long-tailed, brightly colored birds which live on insects caught in flight in flycatcher fashion. Motmots are solitary in habits. They nest in cavities in either trees or banks.

Blue-crowned motmot

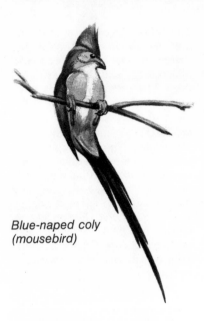

*Blue-naped coly
(mousebird)*

etc. Striped muscles occur in two forms with different physiological properties: 1) the white muscles which can perform fast movements but only over a short period of time and 2) red muscles which have more sustained strength. Thus the pectoral muscles (the breast) of the domestic chicken consist mainly of white fibers, whereas the legs contain mainly red fibers.

Certain muscles are especially well developed in birds in adaptation to the power of flight. Most prominent are the pectoral muscles (the breast) which effectuate the strongest downward movement of the wing. In swimming and terrestrial birds the leg muscles are particularly well developed.

MOUSEBIRD: a member of the family Coliidae. The six species of mousebirds are medium-sized, crested and very long-tailed, grayish-brown birds. They inhabit semi-open country in the southern half of Africa. The bill and legs are short. They are sociable in habits and are usually met with in flocks. A characteristic habit is that they often sleep hanging upside down. They live on vegetable matter, fruits, seeds, and buds.

MUDNEST-BUILDERS: a term sometimes used for the family of *magpie-larks*.

MUSCLES are composed of cells which can contract and therefore effectuate movement. Special muscles are found in blood vessels, the heart, the intestines and several other organs. The skeletal muscles are also called striped muscles and are the muscles which effectuate flight, running,

MYNAH: a member of the family of *starlings*. Mynahs are particularly known for their ability in *mimicry* and are able to imitate human voices.

Common mynah

Clark's nutcracker

NAPE: the upper part of the hind neck situated right behind the area known as the crown.

NAVIGATION: the ability of a bird to find its way from one point to the other without visual landmarks: *orientation*.

NERVOUS SYSTEM: receives the stimuli from the environment and integrates the various activities of the body. The nervous system is divided into the peripheral nervous system and the central nervous system.

The peripheral nerves consist of the nerves conducting sensory impulses from skin, muscles, internal organs, etc., to the spinal cord and brain, as well as the nerves which supply the muscles necessary for activity. Internal organs and blood vessels are supplied by the autonomic nervous system which influences their activity. Of special interest are the nerves entering the brain from special sense organs such as the *eye* and the *ear*. These are highly developed in birds which rely largely on visual and auditory stimuli.

The central nervous system consists of the spinal cord, the brain stem, the cerebellum and the

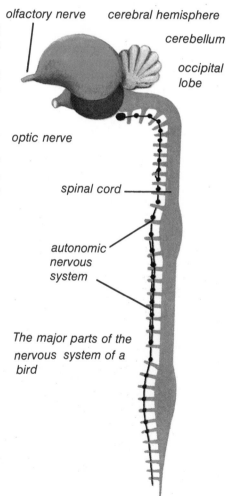

olfactory nerve   cerebral hemisphere

cerebellum

occipital lobe

optic nerve

spinal cord

autonomic nervous system

The major parts of the nervous system of a bird

133

cerebral hemispheres. Although many reflexes do not reach higher levels than the spinal cord, the main function of the spinal cord is that of mediating impulses to and from higher integrative centers. In the brain stem are found centers for such vital functions as breathing and maintenance of normal blood pressure. The cerebellus, or hind brain, which in birds is extremely large, is the integrative organ concerned with the maintenance of balance and coordination. The development of the very large cerebellus in birds is caused by the high demand for coordination in flight. In the cerebral hemispheres the occipital lobes are comparatively large, corresponding well with the bird's high dependence on visual stimuli as this part of the brain receives the fibers from the eye. Other parts of the cerebral hemispheres are much less developed than in mammals, corresponding with the limited capacity for learning in birds compared with mammals.

NEST: a structure built by a bird, or a spot where the eggs are laid and incubated.

The site chosen for the placement of the nest varies tremendously from species to species; some birds dig nest burrows into the ground, some nest on the ground, some in trees and bushes, some nest on cliff ledges, etc. Within a given species, however, the choice of nest sites is fairly constant, although it might be modified by local circumstances. Thus kittiwakes (a kind of gull) usually nest on ledges or cliffs, but may nest on roofs or even among large boulders in certain areas. Differences in nest sites may also be found within the same species in different geographical areas. For instance, the brown thrasher nests in bushes in eastern North America, but on the ground in the western parts.

The nest site may be selected by the female alone or, more rarely, by the male alone. It is most common, however, that both sexes participate in the selection of the nesting site. Often the male will have selected several different sites from which the female makes her choice.

The nest itself may be built by

Cross section of nest

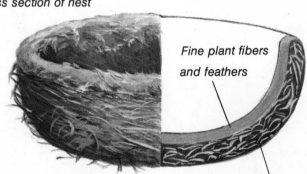

Fine plant fibers and feathers

mud mixed with grass

Grey woodpecker

Swallow

Reed warbler

Tailor bird

Cassins malambe

Blackbird

Golden eagle

Common tern

Oriole

Horned grebe

both sexes, each participating equally, or the nest may be built by the female alone or by the male alone. In the latter two cases the other partner might contribute to the gathering of material for the nest. In yet other species no nest is built at all, the egg being merely laid at the site selected.

The time required for the completion of the nest depends largely on the complexity of the structure itself. Most passerines are able to build their nest in less than a week. Some species, particularly large birds of prey, may use the same nest year after year, but this is the exception rather than the rule. Usually several different types of material are used in the construction of the nest. Coarser branches or leaves are used on the outside, finer plant fibers on the inside. Many species make the nest sturdier by the use of clay either on the exterior of the nest (swallows), or between the layers of twigs (thrushes). Feathers and down are often used to help insulate the nest. Some species of swift use saliva for the construction of their nests which are half-cups glued to the vertical surface of a cave or hollow tree. Some of these nests are *edible nests*. Some birds, for instance terns, use hardly any nest material at all, a mere scraping in the sand sufficing. Other species, for instance the tailor birds, sew leaves together to form the basis for their nests.

Weaver finches build highly intricate structures, sometimes with several chambers for each nest. Grebes build floating nests which are anchored to nearby reeds or other vegetation. Some megapodes build elaborate mounds where the fermenting plant material supplies the heat necessary for the incubation of the eggs. Birds nesting in holes may either construct a cavity themselves, for instance kingfishers which dig burrows in banks, or woodpeckers which chisel the nest cavity out of a tree, or they may use pre-existing cavities (starlings, house sparrows, titmice, owls, etc.). Some birds build no nest at all, namely the so-called *parasitic birds*. Best known among these are the cuckoos, the parasitic weaver birds and cowbirds.

NEST BOX: a man-made structure designed to attract hole-nesting birds. It is synonymous with *birdhouse*.

NESTLING: a term used for a young bird which has not yet left the nest.

NEW WORLD SEED-EATER: a member of the family Fringillidae. With its 315 species this family is one of the largest. It includes such groups as *buntings, cardinals, finches* and *sparrows*. They are small, rather thick-billed birds found throughout most of the world

White crowned sparrow

Black-headed grosbeak

European goldfinch

with the exception of Australia, New Zealand and the Antarctic. Whereas the cardinals, buntings and finches are usually brightly colored, the sparrows are mainly brown or gray. Many species are quite gregarious outside the breeding season, but solitary nesters. They live mainly on seeds, and members of the family may be found in almost any habitat.

NEW WORLD VULTURE: member of the family Vulturidae. The seven species of these vultures are limited in distribution to North, Central and South America. They are large, soaring birds of prey and included in the family is the largest flying bird, the California condor. Their heads and necks are bare. The plumage is usually black with white markings. New World vultures are mainly carrion eaters. They nest in tree or rock cavities. The North American representatives of the family are the California condor, turkey vulture and black vulture.

NEW WORLD WARBLER: alternative name for a member of the family of *wood warblers*.

Turkey vulture

King vulture

137

New Zealand rock wren

NEW ZEALAND WREN: member of the family Acanthisittidae. The three species are limited to New Zealand where they inhabit woods and semiopen country. They are very small, short-tailed and short-winged, brownish or greenish birds which find their insect food on branches or among rocks. They nest in cavities.

NICTITATING MEMBRANE: a transparent membrane between the eyelids and the cornea. It can be pulled across the eye horizontally without shutting off all light.

Nicitating membrane half closed

Nicitating membrane closed

NIDIFUGOUS: a term referring to a young bird that leaves the nest very soon after hatching.

NIGHTJAR: a term used for some members of the family of *goatsuckers*.

NOCTURNAL: active at night. Only relatively few birds are nocturnal in their habits. These include members of the families of *owls, goatsuckers,* and *kiwis*. Many more birds are active both during the day and at night. This is particularly true of waterfowl and shorebirds.

NOMENCLATURE: the scientific naming of the various subspecies, species, genera, families and other groups of birds, mainly used in *taxonomy*. The nomenclature of birds follows the International Code of Zoological Nomenclature. It is based on the *binominal system* according to which each species is identified by two names: the first one refers to the genus, the second identifies the species within the genus. In cases where a

An engraving of Linneaus

Whooping cranes

species is divided into several subspecies a trinominal system is used, the third name identifying the subspecies. Closely related genera of birds are grouped into families, the scientific names of which have the ending "idae." Closely related families are then grouped into orders which have the ending "iformes." The scientific names chosen for a given species follow the rule of priority according to which the oldest available name after the publication of *Systema Naturae* by Linnaeus in 1758 has priority over all the other names.

NONPASSERINE: a species of bird belonging to an order other than that of the Passeriformes.

NUMBERS: About 8,700 different species of birds inhabit the world. These species are not evenly distributed and many more species are found in tropical regions than in the temperate zones. There are, for instance, about 700 different species of birds found in North America north of the Mexican border, but more than 2,900 in South America. What the colder areas of the world lack in diversity is made up by the number of individuals. Out of an estimated 100 billion birds inhabiting the world North America has been estimated to harbor 20 billion, or 20 per cent. As the land area is about 17 per cent of the total land mass of the world, this indicates a fairly even distribution of individuals.

For each individual species the total *population* varies from the very small populations of such species as the whooping crane (about 50) to the hundreds of millions of queleas found in Africa.

NUPTIAL: plumage and behavior related to the breeding season.

Red-breasted nuthatch

NUTHATCH: member of the family Sittidae. The twenty-seven species of nuthatches are small woodpecker-like birds. They are found on all continents with the exception of Antarctica and South America. Most of the nuthatches inhabit woodland, but a few species may be found in rocky, barren country. Gray, black and brown are the dominant colors in most species. Nuthatches are solitary in habits. They nest in cavities. The North American representatives of the family are the white-breasted, red-breasted, brown-headed and pigmy nuthatch.

NUTTALL, THOMAS (1786–1859): outstanding American botanist and ornithologist after whom a woodpecker is named.

European nuthatch

Brown-headed nuthatch

Pygmy owl

OBSERVATORY: a station for the observation of bird *migration*. Observatories are usually placed on islands or along coastlines where migrating birds concentrate. They are often equipped with traps and nets for the purpose of *banding* birds. Some of the most famous observatories are found on Heligoland in the North Sea, Fair Isle and Skokholm of the British Isles and Rossitten on the Baltic coast.

OILBIRD: the single member of the family Steatornithidae. The oilbird is closely related to *goatsuckers*. It is found in semiopen country in the northern part of South America. The oilbird is a large, brown, long-winged bird with a strong hooked bill which is used for picking fruits off different palms. It is nocturnal in its habits, spending the daylight hours in deep caves. Oilbirds are very gregarious and caves may harbor hundreds of birds. The nestlings become very fat at one state reaching a weight one and one half times that of the adult. The bird is named from the native habit of collecting young and boiling off the thick layers of fat, which is used in the household.

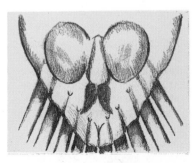

Oil glands on tail (preen gland).

Oil bird

OIL GLAND (or preen gland): secretes an oily substance which is of importance in the maintenance of the *feathers*. The two oil glands are situated just above the root of the tail. They are present in most, but not all, birds and are highest developed in a species leading an aquatic life, such as waterfowl. The

141

When soaked by oil the plumages of birds lose their water resistance.

secretion is expressed with the bill when the bird is *preening* and applied to the feathers. The secretion is usually odorless but in some species, such as the musk duck, it has a strong smell.

OIL POLLUTION has become an increasing danger to water birds with the increasing trade in and consumption of oil in this century. Great spills of oil occur at shipwrecks which may be unavoidable. However, much more menacing is the deliberate washing out of oil tanks at sea by both tankers and other ships. The oil released in the sea floats in a thin layer on top of the heavier water and may cover large parts of the surface. When birds come in contact with this oil, their plumage can no longer be kept water-proof because of the oil sticking to the feathers. They are unable to fly and eventually die. As the oil has a calming effect on the waves the polluted surface often attracts water birds, adding to the disastrous results. Thousands of birds succumb annually because of oil pollution. International efforts have long been made to limit the degree of oil pollution but they have only met with limited success. However, there are hopes that concerted efforts in the future will be more successful as the popular interest in conservation grows.

OLD WORLD FLYCATCHER: member of the family Mucicapidae. The 398 species of Old World flycatchers are distributed through

Eurasia, Africa and Australia. In the New World their ecological niche is occupied by the *tyrant flycatchers*. The Old World flycatchers are small, short-billed birds. In most the tail is of medium length but in some, the paradise flycatchers, the tail is very long. They vary greatly in colors, some, like the red-capped robin of Australia, being very colorful, whereas others, like the spotted flycatcher of Eurasia, are dull gray. Most members of the family are forest dwellers, but some are found in semiopen country. Most live on insects caught in the air as the bird, in a short flight from its perch, captures its prey. They are solitary in habits. Several species are hole-nesters but most build nests in the open.

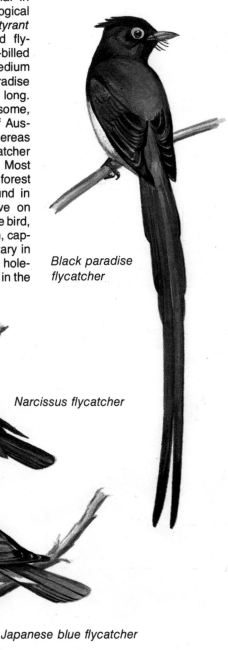

Black paradise flycatcher

Narcissus flycatcher

Japanese blue flycatcher

143

Golden-crowned kinglet

Willow warbler

Sardinia warbler

OLD WORLD WARBLER: member of the family Sylviidae. The 279 species of Old World warblers are small, slender-billed birds, usually quite plainly colored. They are cosmopolitan in distribution and although most are forest dwellers, several species inhabit marshes and open, bushy country. Most are solitary in their habits. The North American representatives of the family are the two kinglets, the golden-crowned and the ruby-crowned. Old World warblers are among the most accomplished singers, the song often being very varied and pleasing in quality. Some, like the marsh warbler, are expert mimics.

OOLOGY: the study of birds' *eggs*. The greatest interest has been in the external appearance of the egg (color, shape, and size). Ooology was quite popular in the latter part of the 19th centruy and the beginning of the 20th, but interest in it has diminished considerably since. Large collections of eggs were assembled. In most countries the collecting of eggs is now illegal because of its threat to particularly endangered species.

ORBITAL: refers to the area surrounding the eye.

ORDERS OF BIRDS

CASSOWAR
AND EM

ORDER: in *taxonomy*, a group of *families*. Various authorities differ in opinion as to the content of various orders. In this book the following orders of living birds are recognized: *Anseriformes, Apodiformes, Apterygiformes, Ardeiformes, Caprimulgiformes, Casuariiformes, Charadriiformes, Coliiformes, Columbiformes, Coraciiformes, Cuculiformes, Falconiformes, Galliformes, Gaviiformes, Gruiformes, Passeriformes, Pelecaniformes, Phoenicopteriformes, Piciformes, Podicipediformes, Procellariiformes, Psittaciformes, Rheiformes, Sphenisciformes, Strigiformes, Struthioniformes, Tinamiformes, Trochiliformes, Trogoniformes.*

HUMMINGBIRDS

TROGONS

PERCHING BIRDS

COLIES

WOODPECKERS AND THEIR ALLIES

KINGFISHERS AND THEIR ALLIES

CUCKOOS AND THEIR ALLIES

GOATSUCKERS AND THEIR ALLIES

PARROTS

SWIFTS

OWLS

SHOREBIRDS GULLS AND AUKS

CRANES, RAILS AND THEIR ALLIES

LOONS

PIGEONS

FOWL-LIKE BIRDS

WATERFOWL

BIRDS-OF-PREY

GREBES

AMOUS

HERONS AND THEIR ALLIES

FLAMINGOES

PELICANS AND THEIR ALLIES

KIWIS

TUBENOSES

OSTRICHES

145

RHEAS

PENGUINS

ORIENTATION: the ability of a bird to determine its geographical position and to move in a fixed direction.

The high level of orientation in birds is remarkable. During migration the individual bird might cover thousands of miles between breeding and wintering grounds and yet, as *banding* has shown, be able to return to the exact spot where it nested the previous year. To investigate the orientation of birds many different experiments have been made. In one kind of experiment a nesting bird is transported to a remote spot and released. The time it takes the bird to return to the nesting site, which is under constant observation, is then measured. Experiments of this nature have shown that a manx shearwater could find its way back across the Atlantic (circa 3,000 miles) in less than two weeks. The Layson albatross has been recorded as traveling 3,200 miles in 10 days. Experiments with land birds have shown similar, although less spectacular, results. This ability to return to a "home site" is the basis for the use of homing pigeons with which many experiments have been conducted, especially trying to determine the method by which the birds orient themselves.

Many theories on the orientation of birds have been advanced. Several of these can be regarded as purely theoretical without any experimental proof. Sensitivity to magnetism, for instance, has not been proven in any animal and attempts to disorient birds by attaching magnets to them have been unsuccessful. Although the recognition of landmarks undoubtedly plays a role in short-distance orientation, it cannot explain the longer travels. Experiments with caged birds exposed to various directions of sunlight (manipulated with the help of mirrors) have, however, shown that many birds are able to orient themselves by the help of the sun. Similar experiments with night migrants exposed to different constellations of stars in planetariums have also shown that many species are capable of orienting themselves by the help of the stars. These experiments concur with the observation that at times when the sky is overcast orientation is often poor. To be able to navigate by the help of the sun and the stars, as sailors have done for centuries, requires a knowledge of time, using a chronometer. It is therefore necessary to postulate that birds posses an "internal clock" enabling them to use the celestial bodies in their navigation. That such an internal clock exists is indeed very likely. Although many aspects of orientation remain unknown, the basic methods are now quite well established.

ORIOLE: member of the family Oriolidae. In North America the term also refers to some members of the family of *icterids*. The 28 species of orioles are found through the southern Palearctic region, but the rest are confined to the tropical parts of the Old World. Orioles are medium-sized, very brightly colored birds with strong pointed bills. They are all forest dwellers that live on fruits and insects. They are solitary in habits.

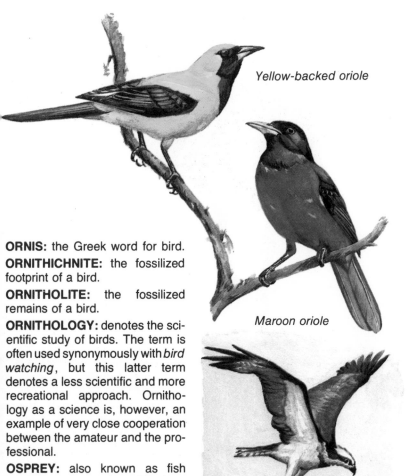

Yellow-backed oriole

Maroon oriole

Osprey

ORNIS: the Greek word for bird.

ORNITHICHNITE: the fossilized footprint of a bird.

ORNITHOLITE: the fossilized remains of a bird.

ORNITHOLOGY: denotes the scientific study of birds. The term is often used synonymously with *bird watching*, but this latter term denotes a less scientific and more recreational approach. Ornithology as a science is, however, an example of very close cooperation between the amateur and the professional.

OSPREY: also known as fish hawk, the sole member of the family Pandionidae. The osprey is a large bird of prey which is generally white below, dark above. It is almost cosmopolitan in its distribution. It lives solely on fish which it grabs with its claws in a headlong dive into the water. Its large nest may be placed in a tree or sometimes on the ground. Ospreys are usually solitary in their habits, although loose colonies near favored fishing grounds may be encountered.

147

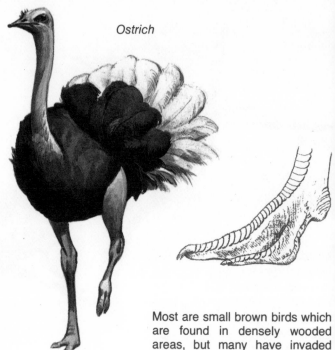

Ostrich

Most are small brown birds which are found in densely wooded areas, but many have invaded other more open habitats. They are usually found near the ground, but some seek food in the forest canopy and others on tree trunks. The family has been named after the nesting habits of many of the species. They build large oven-shaped, domed nests of mud. Other members of the family nest in tree holes, tree cavities, or holes in the ground.

OSTRICH: the single species of the family Struthionidae. The ostrich is the largest of living birds. It may reach a height of 8 feet and weigh almost 350 lbs. The ostrich is a very long-necked and long-legged flightless bird of open country. Its range is restricted to Africa. Ostriches are quite gregarious and usually met with in parties of half a dozen birds. Several females lay their eggs in the same nest, which is attended by both sexes.

OVARY: the female gonad which is part of the *reproductive system*.

OVENBIRD: member of the family Furnariidae. The 215 species of ovenbirds are limited in distribution to Central and South America.

Ovenbird

148

OWL: member of the family Strigidae. The 121 species of owls very in size from 6–30 inches. Members of the family are found on all continents with the exception of Antarctica. Most owls are gray or brown with a very soft plumage. The eyes are usually large, an adaptation to their nocturnal habits. Most owls are hole-nesters, or may use the abandoned nests of other birds. They live on animals ranging in size from small insects to rabbits. Seventeen species represent the family in North America. The more common and widespread species are screech owl, barred owl and saw-whet owl.

Screech owl

Barred owl

Snowy owl

Owlet frogmouth

OWLET FROGMOUTH: member of the family Aegothelidae. The eight species of owlet frogmouths are limited in distribution to Australia and neighboring areas. They are closely related to the *goatsuckers* and, like these, are medium-sized, nocturnal, brownish birds. They nest in tree cavities.

OXPECKER: a term used for two species of the family of *starlings*. Oxpeckers are limited to Africa where they obtain their food by removing ticks from the hides of large animals.

OYSTERCATCHER: member of the family Haematopodidae. The six species of oystercatchers are almost cosmopolitan in their dis-

Oxpeckers on square-lipped rhinoceros

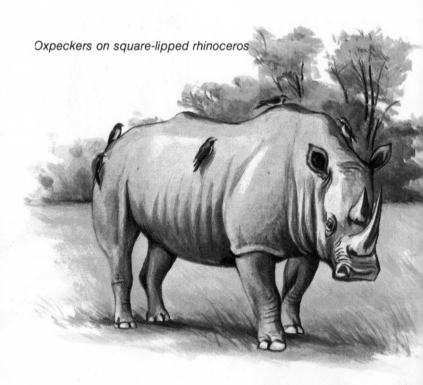

tribution. They inhabit seacoasts, feeding on small mollusks, crustaceans, and sandworms. Oystercatchers are rather large, long-legged and long-billed shorebirds which are either black or black and white in color. Outside the breeding season they are social in habits and often are met with in large flocks. The two North American representatives are the American and the black oystercatcher.

American oystercatcher

Black oystercatcher

P

American white pelican

PAINTED SNIPE: a member of the family Rostratulidae. The two species are found in the tropical part of the Old World and in South America. They are medium-sized shorebirds with shorter bills more boldly patterned brown and white than the true *snipes*. They live in marshes. All parental care is done by the male.

Much more common, though, are pair bonds of longer duration. In most passerines, the pair lasts for the breeding season only and the partners may have new partners the following season. In other species the pair bonds may last until one of the partners dies. One of the many functions of *display*, including *singing*, is the strengthening of the bond of the pair. The formation of the pair may take place on the breeding grounds just prior to the breeding season, or it may occur on the wintering grounds prior to starting migration.

Painted snipe

Palm chat

PAIR: two birds of opposite sex which have mated.

The pair bond may be very short-lived, the only interrelation being copulation. Such is, for instance, the case of several species which perform *lek* display.

PALM CHAT: the single member of the family Dulidae, a medium-sized, brown and striped passerine limited in distribution to the Caribbean Islands. It is a highly social species which nests in large communal nest-structures.

PARASITIC BIRDS: birds which are parasitic in regard to parental care. The eggs of a parasitic species are laid in the nest of another species which then rears the young as its own.

Parasitism has evolved in several families of birds. Among the waterfowl the black-headed duck of South America lays its egg in the nest of coots and other ducks. Several members of the family of *weaver finches* parasitize other members of the family. Among the *icterids* the cowbirds are partially or completely parasitic in their nesting behavior. The *honeyguides* are also parasitic as are many members of the family of *cuckoos*. In some cases the host is able to rear its own young along with the parasite as is, for instance, the case in birds parasitized by the black-headed duck. In others the presence of the parasite greatly decreases the chance of survival of the host species' young as, for instance, in the cowbirds. In the most extreme cases like the cuckoo, the young of the parasite eject the eggs or young of its foster siblings. The cuckoo has further adapted to its parasitic breeding habit by evolving egg colors and patterns, mimicking those of its different hosts.

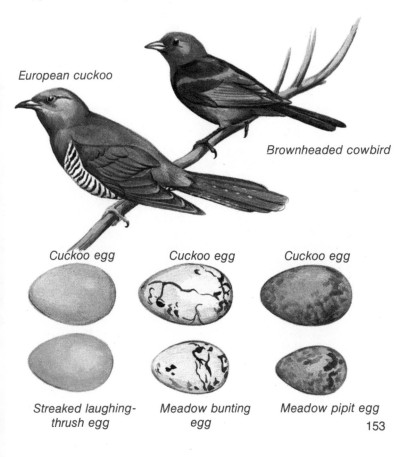

European cuckoo

Brownheaded cowbird

Cuckoo egg *Cuckoo egg* *Cuckoo egg*

Streaked laughing-thrush egg *Meadow bunting egg* *Meadow pipit egg*

153

Turquoise parrot

Yellow-headed conure

PARROT: member of the family Psittacidae. The 317 species of parrots are found throughout the tropical and subtropical regions of the world. They vary in size from 4 to 40 inches. They are colorful birds, many with very brilliant color combinations and most with rather long tails. The bill is short and strong and markedly hooked. Most parrots are forest dwellers which move among the branches using their bill as a third leg to aid in the climbing. Some, however, are found in open country. This is particularly true of the Australian parakeets. Parrots live on fruits, berries and seeds. Although most are solitary in their habits, others, like the budgerigar of Australia, are extremely social in their habits. Parrots are hole-nesters, most using tree cavities, but others burrow in the ground. The only North American parrot, the Carolina parakeet, has become extinct.

PARROTBILL: a member of the family Panuridae. The nineteen species of parrotbills are found in semiopen and open country in Eurasia. They are small, strong-billed, rather plain-colored passerines which are social in habits. The bearded tit, found in Europe and Asia, differs from typical parrotbills by having a small bill and rather strong plumage patterns.

PASSAGE MIGRANT: a bird which occurs in a certain area during migration only.

Yellow-naped Amazon parrot

Fischers lovebird

African
grey parrot

Golden-
mantled
rosella

Hooded parrot

Dusky parrot

PASSERIFORMES: the largest order of birds comprising more than half of all species. These are divided into the families of *accentor, antbird, asity, babbler, bell magpie, bird of paradise, bowerbird, broadbill, bulbul, cotinga, creeper, crow, cuckoo shrike, dipper, drongo, flower-pecker, gnatcatcher, goldfinch, Hawaiian honeycreeper, helmet shrike, honey-eater, hypocholius, icterid, lark, leafbird, lyrebird, manakin, mimine thrush, mudnest-builder, New World seed-eater, New Zealand wren, nuthatch, Old World flycatcher, Old World warbler, oriole, ovenbird, palm chat, parrotbill, pepper-shrike, pipit, pitta, plantcutter, plush-capped finch, scrubbird, sharpbill, shrike, shrike vireo, silky flycatcher, starling, sunbird, swallow, swallow tanager, tanager, tapaculos, thrush, titmouse, treecreeper, tyrant flycatcher, vanga shrike, wattlebird, waxbill, waxwing, weaverfinch, whistler, whiteeye, woodcreeper, wood swallow, wood-warbler, wren, wrentit, wrenwarbler.*

This large order is also the highest developed order of birds.

PASSERINE: a species belonging to the order *Passeriformes*. Passerines are generally small- to medium-sized perching birds.

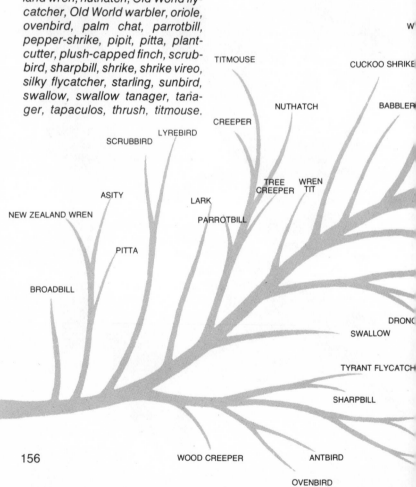

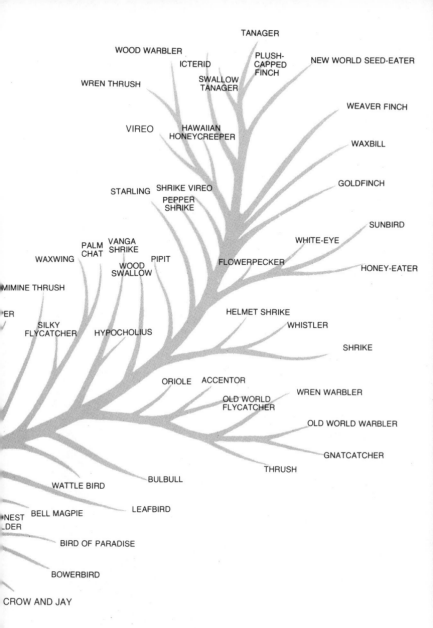

FAMILY TREE OF PASSERINES

TANAGER

WOOD WARBLER

ICTERID

PLUSH-CAPPED FINCH

NEW WORLD SEED-EATER

SWALLOW TANAGER

WREN THRUSH

WEAVER FINCH

VIREO

HAWAIIAN HONEYCREEPER

WAXBILL

GOLDFINCH

STARLING

SHRIKE VIREO

PEPPER SHRIKE

SUNBIRD

VANGA SHRIKE

PALM CHAT

WHITE-EYE

WAXWING

PIPIT

FLOWERPECKER

HONEY-EATER

WOOD SWALLOW

MIMINE THRUSH

HELMET SHRIKE

WHISTLER

ER

SILKY FLYCATCHER

HYPOCHOLIUS

SHRIKE

ORIOLE

ACCENTOR

WREN WARBLER

OLD WORLD FLYCATCHER

OLD WORLD WARBLER

GNATCATCHER

THRUSH

BULBULL

WATTLE BIRD

LEAFBIRD

NEST
_DER

BELL MAGPIE

BIRD OF PARADISE

BOWERBIRD

CROW AND JAY

TCUTTER

NGA

AKIN

CULOS

PECKING ORDER: refers to the hierarchy of *dominance* found in some species of birds living in flocks, as well as among caged birds. This was first described in domestic chickens.

PECTEN: part of the *eye* unique to birds.

PELAGIC BIRDS: those which live most of their lives on the open sea beyond the continental shelf. Virtually all truly pelagic species belong to the order *Procellarii-formes*. Many ocean birds inhabiting the sea over the continental shelves, such as *auks, gannets* and some *gulls,* are sometimes included in the term.

PELICANIFORMES: an order of swimming birds having all four toes webbed. The order contains the families of *anhinga, cormorant, frigate bird, gannet, pelicans* and *tropic-birds*.

PELICAN: a member of the family Pelecanidae. The six species of pelicans are found on all continents except Antarctica. They live in lakes or along seashores. Pelicans are very large, broad-winged birds with a very long bill, the lower part of which possesses a large pouch. Five are black and white, one brown. They are social in habits and nest in large colonies. Their food consists of fish caught either by diving or scooping with the pouch. The two North American representatives of the family are the white pelican and the brown pelican.

Brown pelican

158

PELLET: indigestible food items which are regurgitated. Many species of birds cast up pellets but the habit is particularly common among owls and birds of prey where the pellet will contain bones, hair and feathers of the prey swallowed. Pellets cast up by herons and other fish-eating birds contain scales and bones of fish.

PENGUIN: a member of the family Spheniscidae. The fifteen living species of penguins are limited in distribution to the shores of the Southern Hemisphere. They are medium-sized to large, black and white diving birds with strong bills. All have lost the power of flight and the wings are adapted for swimming. They are expert divers which live on fish caught under water. On land they walk in an upright position. Penguins nest in colonies,

Rockhopper penguin

Emperor penguin

Adelie penguin

some species in burrows. The emperor penguin, which may weigh up to 100 lbs. and stand 3 feet high, breeds in the midst of the Antarctic winter on the ice. The egg rests on the feet of the parent bird and is covered by the abdominal feathers and skin protecting it from the cold.

PEPPER-SHRIKE: a member of the family Cyclarhidae. The two species of pepper-shrikes are found only in Central and South America where they inhabit open woodlands. They are closely related to the *vireos* and like them are rather heavily built, small passerines which move around slowly among the foliage in search for their insect food.

PERCHING BIRDS: refers to the species of the order *Passeriformes*.

PHALAROPE: a member of the family Phalaropodidae, the three species of which inhabit the northern part of the Northern Hemisphere. Phalaropes are small shorebirds which, however, are excellent swimmers. They spend the winter at sea. They are quite brightly colored, black, red and white in the summer plumage, gray and white in winter. The females are more brightly colored than males and the male performs the parental care alone. All three species, northern, red and Wilson's phalarope, are found in North America.

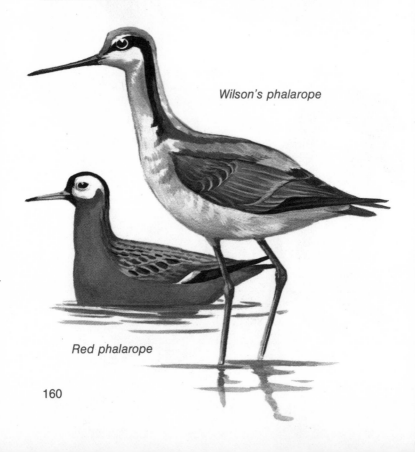

Wilson's phalarope

Red phalarope

Golden pheasant

Swinhoe's pheasant

Himalayan imperial pheasant

PHEASANT: a member of the family Phasianidae. The 177 species of pheasants, which are closely related to *grouse,* vary in size from being small to quite large. They are all ground-dwelling birds, although some may roost in trees. They are mainly plant-eaters, but many supplement the diet with insects and other invertebrates. It is a very diverse family which is divided into several groups. The largest members of the family belong to the group of true pheasants. These are medium-sized to large, very color-ful birds with marked sexual dimorphism. Most are easily domesticated and the red jungle fowl, the ancestor of domestic poultry, belongs to this group. The ring-necked pheasant has been introduced in many parts of the world from its Asiatic homeland. The peacock is another well-known member of this group. The smaller, and usually less colorful, members of the family are known as partridges. Best known and introduced in many areas is the gray partridge which is indigenous to Europe. The so-called francolins found in Africa and Asia are prized game birds belonging to this group. The smallest members of the family, the quails, are divided into two groups, the Old World quail and the New World quail. The Old World quails are very small, almost tailless, short-legged birds, whereas the New World quails generally are larger and often more colorful.

The larger members of the family of pheasants are usually polygamous in breeding habits, whereas the smaller members are monogamous. The family is represented in North America by half a dozen species, including such familiar birds as the bobwhite and the California quail.

Ring-necked pheasant

Grey partridge

Mountain quail

Mourning dove

Yellow-bellied fruit pigeon

Orange dove

Rock dove

PHOENICOPTERIFORMES: an order containing the family of the *flamingos*.

PHOTOPERIODISM: the regulation by light of the cyclical change occurring at the time of *breeding* and *migration*.

PICIFORMES: an order containing the families of *barbets, honeyguides, jacomars, puffbirds, toucans* and *woodpeckers*.

PIGEON: a member of the family Columbidae, many of which are also called doves. The 284 species of pigeons and doves are found throughout the world, with the exception of Antarctica. They are medium-sized, usually very colorful birds with rather weak bills. Most species are found in forests but several have adapted to the open country. They live on seeds, fruits and berries. Many species are very social in habits, the most spectacular example being that of the now extinct passenger pigeon which occurred in North America in flocks numbering millions. Eight indigenous and three introduced species of pigeons occur in North America. They include such well-known birds as the mourning dove, rock dove and the band-tailed pigeon.

PINIONING: the method of rendering a captive bird flightless by cutting the wing at the carpal joint.

Sprague's pipit

PIPIT: a member of the family Motacillidae which also includes the *wagtails*. Pipits are small, rather long-tailed passerines which are usually brown and streaked. They are terrestrial birds of the open country and are world-wide in distribution. They live on insects. The water pipit and Sprague's pipit are representatives of the family in North America.

PIRATIC BIRDS: birds which habitually rob other birds of their food. Although the act of piracy can be observed in a multitude of species, it has only developed to

a high degree in a few. Examples of the latter are the *frigate birds* which rob gannets, gulls, pelicans and other fish-eating birds of their food. In *jaegers* this habit is also highly developed, the victims being mainly different gulls and auks. The African fish eagle obtains most of its food by robbing other fish-eating birds.

Steere's pitta

PITTA: a member of the family Pittidae. Twenty-three species of pittas are found in the tropical parts of the Old World where they inhabit woods and brushlands. They are

Frigatebird chasing brown pelican

Rufous-tailed plantcutter

where the wings are very broad. These are known as lapwings. Outside the breeding season the plovers are social in their habits. Several species have characteristic black neck-bands. The family includes such North American species as the killdeer, the black-bellied plover and the semi-palmated plover.

rather small, very short-winged and short-tailed, colorful passerines which find their food on the ground.

PLANTCUTTER: a member of the family Thytotomidae. The three species of plantcutters are limited in distribution to South America. They are rather long-tailed, finch-like birds with a strong conical bill. They live on fruits and buds.

PLOVER: a member of the family Charadriidae. The sixty-three species of plovers are small- to medium-sized shorebirds with short bills. They have a world-wide distribution, excepting Antarctica. Plovers are generally black and white. The wings are long and pointed except in some species

Snowy plover

Golden plover

Bar-tailed godwit

Summer

Winter

PLUMAGE: the feather covering of a bird. Besides protecting and insulating the body, the feathers make it possible for birds to fly. The different colors make it possible to identify different species and even individual birds. The plumage of a bird changes with age through *molts*. The first plumage is the natal plumage which consists of down feathers. This is soon replaced by the juvenile plumage which often consists of rather loose-structured feathers. This is again lost after a rather short period and replaced with the first winter plumage. This plumage is retained until the time just prior to the following breeding season when, in most passerines, it is replaced by the first nuptial plumage. After the breeding season the winter plumage is again attained. Throughout their adult life most birds have two different plumages, a nuptial or breeding plumage and a winter plumage. In some male ducks an eclipse plumage is acquired shortly after the breeding season has started. This plumage closely resembles that of the female and actually corresponds to the winter plumage of most other birds.

PLUSH-CAPPED FINCH: the sole member of the family Catambly-rhynchidae. The plush-capped

Plush-capped finch

finch is a small, mainly brown and black bird inhabiting northern South America. It owes its name to a peculiar velvetlike cap of orange feathers.

PODICIPEDIFORMES: an order containing the sole family of *grebes*.

POLYANDRY: the establishment of a sexual relationship between a female and more than one male. The term is usually restricted to species where the female, after copulation and the laying of the eggs, no longer participates in the incubation or parental care, but instead moves to establish a sexual relationship with another male. Polyandry is rare among birds and limited to such species as the rhea and some tinamous and a few other species. It is a type of *polygamy*.

POLYGAMY: the establishment of a sexual relationship of a female and more than one male, *polyandry*, or between a male and more than one female, *polygyny*.

POLYGYNY: the establishment of a sexual relationship of one male with more than one female. Polygyny is quite common among birds. It is found widely in such families as *pheasants* and *grouse* where it may take the form of *lek* display. It is also found in several kinds of wrens and icterids.

POPULATION: the total number of a species in a certain area. The size of the world population varies from being extremely small in such threatened species as the whooping crane (about 50 individuals) to the millions of, for instance, the red-winged blackbirds inhabiting North America. The exact world

The redwing is one of the most numerous birds in North America.

population is known for only few species. The population of the California condor is about 60, of the Kirtland's warbler about 800, to mention two North American examples. Larger populations of more common birds cannot be exactly known but only estimated. In trying to make such estimations various methods of *census*-taking are employed.

Great potoo

POTOO: a member of the family Nyctibiidae. The five species of potoos are closely related to the *goatsuckers*. They are rather large brown, nocturnal forest birds, limited in distribution to the West Indies, Central and South America. They catch their insect food in flycatcher fashion.

POWDER DOWN: specialized *feathers* which give off a powder used for the cleansing of the plumage. These specialized feathers are found in such birds as herons, toucans and parrots.

PRATINCOLE: a member of the subfamily Glareolinae which together with *coursers* forms the family Glareolidae. The seven species of pratincoles are found in

Pratincole

most of the warmer parts of the Old World. They are very long-winged, short-legged and short-billed shorebirds which live on insects caught in the air. Most are of the size of a thrush and quite social in habits.

PRECOCIAL: term referring to a young bird capable of locomotion immediately after hatching.

PREENING: the cleaning and arrangement of the feathers by the bill. Birds spend long periods of time preening. This, together with other feather maintenance behavior in the form of bathing, oiling, dusting, anting, etc., keeps the individual feathers in the proper order and the plumage intact.

Preening

PRIMARY FEATHERS: the outer flight *feathers* attached to the hand.

PROCELLARIIFORMES: an order containing the family of *albatrosses, diving petrels, shearwaters* and *storm petrels.*

PSITTACIFORMES: an order comprising the single family of the parrots.

PSITTACOSIS: a virus disease affecting, not only parrots, but also several other species of birds, and transmittable to man in whom it takes the form of an atypical pneumonia.

PTERYLOSIS: the distribution of feathers on the skin of the bird, usually in feather tracts.

PUFFBIRD: a member of the family Bucconidae. The thirty species of puffbirds are limited in their distribution to Central and South America where they inhabit wood-

Collared puffbird

land. They are medium-sized, rather dull-colored brown birds with a large head and strong bill somewhat reminiscent of the tyrant flycatchers. They live on insects caught in flycatcher fashion. They nest in cavities.

169

Quail

Q

QUAIL: term used for the members of two different groups of the family of *pheasants*. The Old World quails are very small, chubby, terrestrial birds distributed through most of the Old World. The New World quails are generally larger and more brightly colored. They are distributed throughout most of the New World and include such species as the bobwhite and the California quail.

QUELEA: a member of the family of *weaver finches*, also called red-billed dioch, which is a major crop pest in the southern parts of Africa. The quelea is one of the most numerous birds, the total population numbering hundreds of millions of birds. The destruction of grain crops by queleas has caused major famines in local areas. Queleas are extremely social in their habits and nest in enormous colonies. Attempts at controlling the damage by destroying the birds with poison, flame throwers, explosives, etc., have met with virtually no success.

QUETZAL: one of the members of the family of *Trogons*, limited in distribution to Central America, and the national bird of Guatemala. The quetzal was held sacred by the ancient Maya Indians.

QUILL: term used for a stiff feather (*remex* and *rectrix*) and sometimes used to denote the calamus, the nude part of the shaft of a feather.

Quetzal

R

Swallow-tailed indian roller

RACE: term used synonymously with *subspecies*.

RACHIS: the distal part of the shaft of a *feather* supporting the vanes.

RAIL: any of a group of birds which together with the *coots* and *gallinules* form the family *Rallidae*. The 120 species of rails, coots and gallinules inhabit wetlands throughout the world excepting the polar regions.

Rails are small to medium-sized birds with rather long legs and toes and long bills. Their bodies are compressed laterally, allowing them to slip through dense vegetation with ease. The colors are mainly gray, black and brown. The wings are short and rounded. The flight is weak, and several island species have completely lost the power of flight. Some of the smaller, more short-billed rails are called crakes. An example is the corn crake of Eurasia which differs from other rails by inhabiting dry grassland rather than marshes and swamps. The six species found in North America are the clapper, king, Virginia, sora, yellow and black rails.

Purple gallinule

Sora rail

Gallinules differ from the rails by being mainly black and blue in color and having a frontal shield over their short, stocky bill. They are less secretive in behavior than the rails. Coots resemble gallinules but have lobed toes. They swim well and obtain most of their food by diving. Common and purple gallinules are found in North America, as is the American coot.

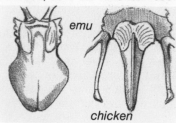
emu

chicken

RATITE: a bird lacking the keel of the breastbone. Ratites are large, flightless, running birds, including the members of the orders Struthioniformes, Rheiformes, Casuariiformes and Apterygiformes.

RECTRIX: a tail *feather*.

REDIRECTION: a term used in behavior denoting a response to an object other than the normal one. An example is the pecking on inedible objects by hungry birds, and the attack during a hostile encounter between birds on a third bird or on a totally unrelated object.

REFLEX: an inborn, immediate response to a certain sensory stimulus.

REFUGE: an area set aside and managed for the protection and preservation of wildlife; a sanctuary. Wildlife refuges play an important role in *conservation*. They may vary in size from a small pond to thousands of acres of land or marshes. According to their main function, refuges can be divided into several categories. Among the largest are big-game refuges, which also benefit resident and migratory birds although they are primarily managed for mammals. Big-game refuges are found on all continents, but Africa contains by far the most spectacular.

Waterfowl refuges are of special importance as wetlands have been destroyed at an increasing rate in attempts to create more agricultural areas. Waterfowl refuges may be situated in the breeding areas, such as Lake Mývatn in Iceland, along the migratory routes of waterfowl, or on wintering grounds such as the Aransas refuge in Texas. These refuges are much needed sanctuaries offering food and protection for large parts of the waterfowl population throughout

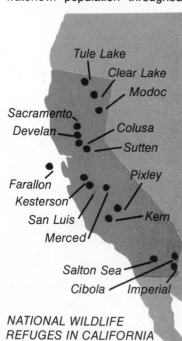
Tule Lake
Clear Lake
Modoc
Sacramento
Develan
Colusa
Sutten
Farallon
Pixley
Kesterson
San Luis
Kern
Merced
Salton Sea
Cibola
Imperial

NATIONAL WILDLIFE REFUGES IN CALIFORNIA

the year. Although primarily oriented toward game birds, they are obviously of great importance for other species in maintaining certain habitats. Refuges set aside for colonially nesting birds have been very successful. In this way colonies of herons, gulls, auks, gannets, etc., are protected during the breeding seasons.

The first national wildlife refuge established in the United States was that of Pelican Island on the Florida coast, set aside on March 14, 1903, for the protection of a colony of brown pelicans. National parks clearly fall within the system of refuges and have proved invaluable in the protection of birds.

RELEASER: a special feature either in the form of shape, color, movement or sound which transmits a stimulus triggering a particular pattern of innate *behavior*. An example of releasers is the black mustachial stripe of the male yellow-shafted flicker which in the breeding season releases courtship in the female and aggressive behavior in males. The red spot on the lower mandible of the herring gull releases food-begging behavior in the young. Many brightly colored parts of plumage as well as the postures during *display* function as releasers, as does *singing*.

REMEX: a flight *feather*. The remiges are usually divided into the primaries, which are attached to the hand, and the secondaries, which are attached to the forearm.

REPRODUCTIVE SYSTEM: In the female bird the reproductive organs consist of one ovary and one oviduct which opens into the *cloaca*. Although the embryo has paired ovaries and oviducts, the ones on the right side usually disappear before hatching. The ovary is situated high on the back wall of the abdominal cavity. In the early breeding season the ovary can be seen to contain many large follicles containing the egg with its yolk. When the egg is released by the ovary, it enters the trumpetlike opening of the oviduct. As it passes through the oviduct, the egg white is secreted and sur-

The red spot on the bill of the herring gull and the black mustachial stripe of the tellow-shafted flicker are both releasers.

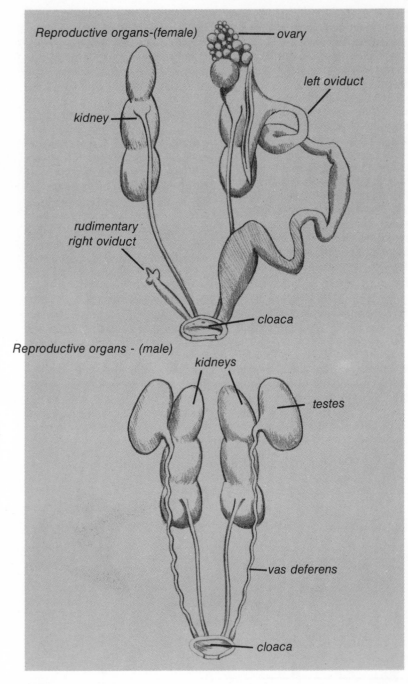

Reproductive organs-(female)

ovary

left oviduct

kidney

rudimentary
right oviduct

cloaca

Reproductive organs - (male)

kidneys

testes

vas deferens

cloaca

rounds the yolk, and later the membranes are formed. In the uterus, the lower part of the oviduct, the eggshell is formed together with its pigments and the pattern.

The male reproductive organs consist of two testes situated in the back upper part of the abdominal cavity from which the different ducts lead to the cloaca. In some families of birds a penislike copulatory organ is found. This is true of the ratites as well as of waterfowl. During copulation this organ is protruded into the cloaca of the female and the sperm deposited. In most birds, however, such an organ does not exist and the sperm flows through the male cloaca into the female cloaca which are closely joined during *copulation*.

The size of the testes varies considerably according to the season and is enormously increased prior to breeding.

RESIDENT: a bird which remains within its breeding area throughout the year.

RESPIRATORY SYSTEM: In birds the respiratory system is very highly developed. It stretches from the nasal opening to the lungs and the air sacs. From the nasal cavities and the mouth the air passes into the larynx and then into the trachea, which is situated in the neck and the upper part of the thoracic cavity. The trachea varies greatly in size and in some species forms large coils or loops which may lodge in excavations of the breastbone. In the trachea the voice organ, the *syrinx*, is found.

Respiratory system of pigeon

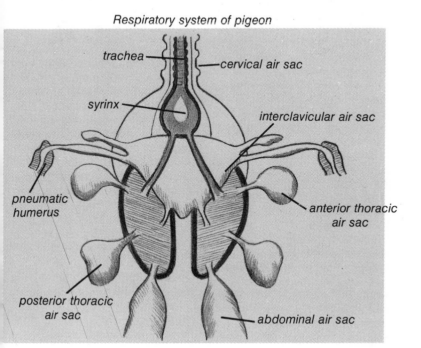

trachea — cervical air sac

syrinx — interclavicular air sac

pneumatic humerus — anterior thoracic air sac

posterior thoracic air sac — abdominal air sac

Rhea male

female

The trachea divides to form two bronchi which further divide, entering the lungs which are situated in the chest cavity. Openings lead from the lungs to the air sacs which may extend into the bones and the abdominal cavity. In the lungs oxygen is taken up by the blood flowing through the capillaries and carbon dioxide is released.

Birds do not have a muscular diaphragm, and the respiratory movements are effectuated by other muscles. During flight the flight muscles perform these functions and respiration is synchronous with the wingbeats. Besides its importance in the gaseous exchange, the respiratory system also plays a prominent role in *heat regulation* as birds do not possess sweat glands. By increasing their respiratory rate birds are able to decrease their body temperature.

RHEA: a member of the family Rheidae which contains only two living species. Rheas are large, flightless long-legged and long-necked birds which may stand up to 5 feet high. They are grayish brown in color. Rheas are limited in distribution to the southern half of South America where they inhabit open plains. They are social in their behavior and are usually met with in flocks of ten to thirty birds. Several females will lay eggs in the same nest which is tended by the male only.

RHEIFORMES: an order of birds containing the single living family of *rheas*.

RIDGWAY, ROBERT (1850– 1929): American ornithologist

whose greatest work was *Birds of North and Middle America* which was published from 1901–1919. A whippoorwill is named after him.

RINGING: synonymous with *banding*.

RITUALIZATION: a term used in the study of *behavior* to denote the development of primitive and stereotype patterns of behavior into more highly complex activities, in which the individual components no longer serve their original function. In most birds *display* consists of components of, for instance, preening, feeding, etc., which have been ritualized.

RIVOLI, DUC de, FRANÇOIS VICTOR MASSÉNA (1799–1863): French nobleman and amateur naturalist who was a friend of J. J. Audubon. A hummingbird is named after him.

ROATELO: a member of the family Mesitornithidae. The three species of roatelos inhabit woods and shrubland of Madagascar. They are medium-sized, long-tailed, ground-dwelling brown birds.

ROLLER: a member of the family Coraciidae. The eleven species of rollers inhabit forest and open woodlands of the warmer parts of the Old World. They are medium-sized, somewhat crowlike birds with brilliant blue and green plumage. They live on insects and small animals caught in the air or on the ground. During the courtship display rollers perform elaborate aerial maneuvers.

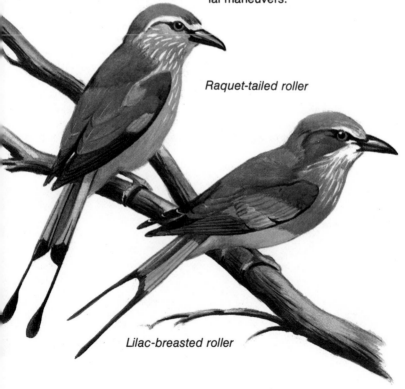

Raquet-tailed roller

Lilac-breasted roller

ROOKERY: a colony of birds. The term comes from the colonies of rooks, members of the crow family, common in Europe.

Rooks

ROOST: a perch or small area where one or more birds are found *roosting*.

ROOSTING: a term used to denote the sleeping of birds. The roosting behavior of birds varies from species to species. Some may roost singly and others in large aggregations in favorite areas. Some species, especially hole-nesting kinds like titmice, often roost in tree cavities, while others roost in the open. Several species of wrens build nestlike structures which are used for roosting only. The site selected for roosting is usually one where the bird is at least partially protected from the low temperature of the surroundings and where it is relatively safe from predators.

Many otherwise solitary species may roost together in enormous aggregations outside the breeding season. This is, for instance, true of some of the *icterids* in North America and of many species of *swallows*. Such roosts often contain thousands or even hundreds of thousands of birds and may be composed of several different species. Thus, the starling which in Europe roosts with members of its own species only, often roosts in North America together with grackles, redwings and cowbirds. Herons and ibises may also roost together. The traffic to and from such roosts is among the most spectacular of sights. Favored communal areas for roosting are swamps where the birds are at least partially protected against land-locked predators. The time of day at which regular activity is stopped and roosting begins, and vice versa, varies greatly among different species. Diurnal birds, however, usually seek out their

Ibises flying to night roost

Ibises at roost

roosting spot before the onset of darkness and leave it at daybreak. Some species, for instance soaring birds of prey, do not leave the roost until well after daybreak when thermal updrafts have started forming. Nocturnal birds generally roost during the day.

Most birds roost sitting in the upright position with the feathers somewhat fluffed to decrease their loss of heat. Several roost with the bill tucked underneath the feathers of the back. Often the birds cluster close together to further limit the heat loss. Certain species of parrots hang upside down when roosting.

ROSS, BERNARD ROGAN (1827–1874): Canadian merchant and naturalist after whom a goose is named.

ROSS, SIR JAMES CLARK (1800–1862): British explorer of the Arctic and Antarctic after whom a gull is named.

179

Black skimmer

S

SABINE, SIR EDWARD (1788–1883): English general and physicist after whom a gull is named.

SALT GLAND: part of the *excretory system* situated above the orbit. The two salt glands help in eliminating excess salt from the organism. They are highly developed in seabirds.

SANCTUARY: a term used synonymously with refuge.

SANDGROUSE: a member of the family Pteroclidae. The sixteen species of sandgrouse inhabit open plains of the southern part of Eurasia and Africa. They are medium-sized, long-winged and long-tailed, ground-dwelling birds with very short legs. The plumage is mainly brown or black and white. Sandgrouse are closely related to pigeons and doves and, like these, are social in their habits. One species, Pallas's sandgrouse, is famous for its irruptions from Asia into Europe. In very dry areas the sandgrouse often fly long dis-

Pin-tailed sandgrouse

Pallas sandgrouse

Ruddy turnstone

Semipalmated sandpiper

Stilt sandpiper

Great knot

Lesser yellowleg

tances in huge flocks for the purpose of drinking. They congregate at water holes in thousands. Sandgrouse live on seeds and insects found on the ground.

SANDPIPER: a member of the family Scolopacidae, which also includes such shorebirds as *curlews, snipes,* and *turnstones*. The eighty-two members of the family are cosmopolitan in distribution, excepting Antarctica. They are mainly found along seashores, but many of them nest in inland swamps. They vary in size from small to medium. Most are brown, white, or gray in coloration. They have rather long legs and bills. Curlews are the largest and have long decurved bills. Godwits are generally slightly smaller with straight or slightly upturned bills.

Snipes are medium-sized, long-billed, brown, chubby shorebirds, whereas the sandpipers proper are small. In America they are often called "peeps." In North America the family is represented by such diverse species as the whimbrel (a curlew), Hudsonian godwit, greater and lesser yellowlegs, short-billed and long-billed dowitchers, ruddy turnstone, American woodcock, and common snipe, as well as the very numerous least, semipalmated and western sandpipers.

SAY, THOMAS (1787–1835): American naturalist after whom a phoebe is named.

SCAPULAR: a term used for one of several feathers situated just above the shoulder.

Scapulars

SCOTT, WINFIELD (1786–1866): American general after whom an oriole is named.

SCREAMER: a member of the family Anhimidae. The three species of screamers inhabit marshes and wetlands of South America. They are rather long-legged waterfowl which are black or gray in color. They have prominent spurs on the wings. Screamers are good flyers and are often seen soaring. They are named after their far-reaching calls. Screamers are usually met with in pairs or small flocks.

SCRUB-BIRD: a member of the family Atrichornithidae. The two species of scrub-birds are found in Australia only. They are rather small, long-tailed, short-winged brown passerines which inhabit areas with dense undergrowth. They are solitary and secretive in habits.

SECONDARY: one of the inner flight *feathers* attached to the arm.

SECRETARY BIRD: the single living member of the family Sagittariidae. The secretary bird is a very large, long-legged and long-tailed, crested bird of prey with gray and

Horned screamer

Secretary bird

black plumage. It inhabits open country of Africa where it stalks smaller animals on foot. It is solitary in habits.

SEDENTARY: a term used to denote nonmigratory birds.

SEEDSNIPE: a member of the family Thinocoridae. The four species of seedsnipes inhabit barren regions of westernmost South America. They are small- to medium-sized, plump, ground-dwelling birds with brownish plumage. They are social in habits. They live on seeds.

SENSES: a term referring to vision, hearing, smell, taste and touch. In birds the vision is usually very acute (see *eye*). The hearing is also well developed (see *ear*), whereas the ability to smell appears very limited. The degree of development of taste is probably quite poor in birds, whereas the sense of touch is quite acute.

Least seedsnipe

Crested seriema

SERIEMA: a member of the family Cariamidae. The two species of seriemas are limited in distribution to open and semiopen country of the central part of South America. They are large, long-legged and long-tailed, crested birds. The plumage is brown and gray. The crested seriema is often domesticated in its native area.

SEXUAL DIMORPHISM: the presence of different appearances of male and female of the same age in the same populations. Sexual dimorphism is extremely common among birds. It may take the form of difference in size. Thus, in many species of birds of prey the female is considerably larger than the male. This is considered by some an adaptation enabling the pair to hunt prey of different size. In many members of the families of grouse and pheasant the males are considerably larger than the females. The most common type of dimorphism, however, is found in regard to plumage colors and patterns. Usually the male is more brightly colored than the female, although exceptions, such as the phalaropes, exist. Sexual dimorphism is thought to have developed as a selection against hybridization between similar species, as well as a selection within the species of particularly striking features in the males favored by the females.

SHARPBILL: the single member of the family Oxyruncidae which inhabits the rain forests of Central and South America. The sharpbill is a medium-sized, greenish passerine with a red crest.

Crested sharpbill

Goshawk

male

female

Larger double-collared sunbird

female

male

Sexual dimorphism

male

female

Black grouse

male

Wilson's phalarope

female

male

Pink-footed shearwater

Greater shearwater

SHEARWATER: a member of the family Procellariidae. The fifty-three species of shearwaters are distributed throughout the world's oceans. They are medium-sized to large, long-winged, somewhat gull-like birds closely related to the albatrosses and storm petrels. Plumages are brown, black, or white. Shearwaters are gregarious in their habits during the breeding season. Most nest colonially on islands where they dig underground burrows. They live on fish and plankton caught far out to sea, and outside the breeding season rarely come within sight of shores. The only member of the family which nests in North America is the fulmar. Several other members, however, visit offshore waters. Examples of these are the sooty, greater, slender-billed, and manx shearwaters.

SHEATHBILL: a member of the family Chionididae. The two species of sheathbills inhabit the rocky shores of the Antarctic continent and surrounding islands. Sheathbills are medium-sized, pigeonlike white birds which live on animal matter. They are social in their habits.

Sheathbill

186

SHOEBILL STORK: the single member of the family Balaenicipitidae. The shoebill, or whalehead, stork is found in the marshes of Africa. It is a large, long-legged, long-necked, dark gray bird with a characteristic long and very wide bill. It is solitary in its habits and lives mainly on aquatic animals.

SHOREBIRD: a term used to denote several families of the order *Charadriiformes*.

SHRIKE: a member of the family Laniidae. The sixty-four species of shrikes are distributed throughout most of the world, with the exception of South America and Australia. They inhabit open and semi-open country. They are small- to medium-sized passerines which have a rather large head and a strong hooked bill. In color they vary from black and white patterns to bright red and yellow. Shrikes are solitary in habits. They are pugnacious birds, most of them living on insects, but the larger ones also catching reptiles, mammals and

Shoebill stork

other birds. They often impale their prey on thorns or other spikes. In North America the family is represented by the loggerhead and great northern shrike.

Red-backed shrike

Northern shrike

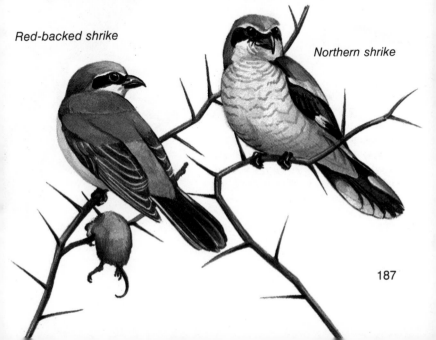

187

Western shrike thrush

SILKY FLYCATCHER: a member of the family Ptilogonatidae. The four species of silky flycatchers are found in southernmost North America and Central America where they inhabit dry semiopen country. They are medium-sized passerines, solid brown or black in color with wing markings. All have a rather prominent crest. The North American representative of the family is the phainopepla.

SINGING: vocalization associated with reproductive behavior, the production of a *song*.

SHRIKE THRUSH: one of two members—the other being the whistler—of the family Pachycephalidae. The forty-two species of the family are found from Australia to the Philippines where they inhabit forests and shrublands. They are small- to medium-sized passerines with strong bills with which they catch insects. Most are solitary in their habits.

Chestnut-sided shrike-vireo

SHRIKE-VIREO: a member of the family Vireolaniidae. The three species of shrike-vireos are limited in distribution to the forests of Central and South America. They are medium-sized, dull greenish or grayish birds but with more striking facial patterns. They are solitary in habits.

Phainopepla

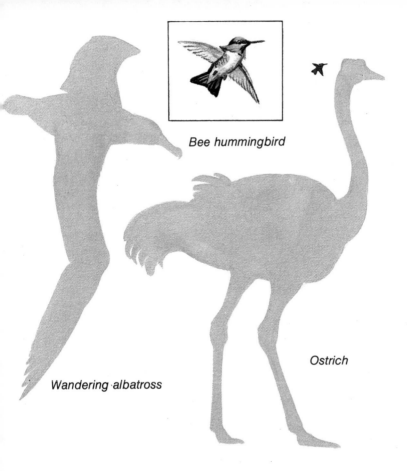

Bee hummingbird

Ostrich

Wandering albatross

SIZE: the total length of a bird from the tip of the bill to the end of the tail. However, size is often also given in reference to weight and wingspread, as well as height when standing.

Birds range in size from the ostrich, which may measure six feet from its bill to the tip of its short tail but may stand as high as eight feet and weigh three hundred pounds, to the bee hummingbird with its length of less than two-and-one-half inches and a weight of about one tenth of an ounce. The largest birds are *flightless*. Of the flying birds, the trumpeter swan, with its length of six feet, wingspan of ten feet, and weight of thirty-eight pounds, is the largest. The largest wingspan recorded—over eleven feet—is that of a wandering albatross.

Within a given species there is often a difference in size between the two sexes. In most cases the male is slightly larger than the female, but in some, for example the turkey, the male is much larger than the female. In certain species of birds of prey the female is considerably larger than the male.

SKELETON: the internal structure of bone and cartilage which protects and supports the other organs of the body.

The vertebrae forming the spinal column in birds are modified and in general are much more rigidly connected than in other vertebrate animals, sometimes even being fused. However, the cervical vertebrae (neck) are separate and quite moveable, allowing for free movement of the head. The vertebrae vary in number largely in accordance with the length of the neck. The ribs are attached to the thoracic vertebrae posteriorly, to the sternum (or breastbone) anteriorly, forming the rib cage in which the lungs and the heart are situated. The sternum is in most birds supplied with a central keel to which the pectoral muscles, which are the main flight muscles, are attached.

Attached to the rib cage is the shoulder girdle consisting of several bones. These support the upper extremity, the wing. The wing consists of the humerus, forming the arm, and the radius and the ulna, forming the forearm. These are attached to the greatly modified carpal bones which in turn attach to the three fingers. The forearm and the hand support the secondary and primary feathers respectively.

At the lower part of the vertebral column the pelvic girdle supports the leg. The leg consists of the femur (or thighbone) and the fibula and tibia, which together form the lower leg. Distally the tibia is fused to the tarsal bones forming the tibiotarsus. The tibiotarsal bone is joined with the metatarsals which are fused into a long slender bone. This bone again supports the toes, which are usually four in number.

The skull, resting on the cervical vertebrae, consists of a large number of fused bones, forming the cranial cavity in which the brain is situated. To it is attached the bill which consists of an upper and a lower mandible.

In general the bird's skeleton is characterized by its extreme lightness, which facilitates flight.

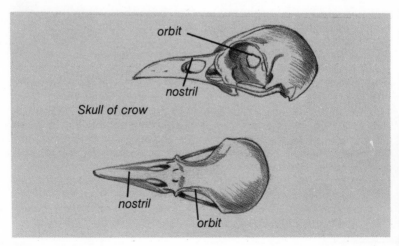

Skull of crow

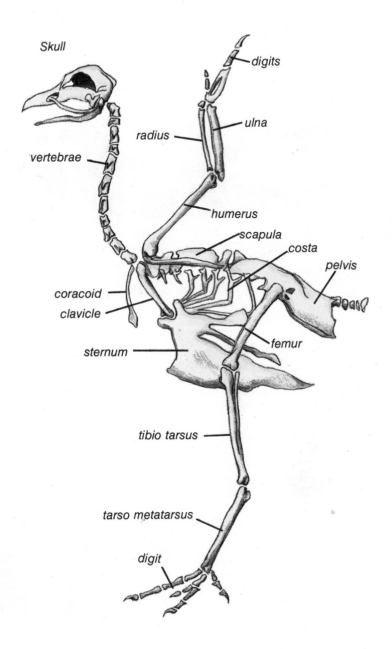

Skull

digits

ulna

radius

vertebrae

humerus

scapula

costa

pelvis

coracoid

clavicle

femur

sternum

tibio tarsus

tarso metatarsus

digit

Skimmers

SKIMMER: a member of the family Rhynchopidae. The three species of skimmers inhabit the Americas, Africa, India and Indo-China. They are found along protected sea-shores, lagoons, large rivers, and lakes. Skimmers are large ternlike black and white birds with a unique bill, in which the lower mandible is considerably longer than the upper mandible. When feeding the skimmers fly low above the water with the lower mandible plowing through the surface. When a prey is encountered, it is picked up by a backward movement of the head and bill. Skimmers are social in habits and nest in large colonies along seashores.

SKUA: name used for two members of the family of *Jaegers*.

SMITH, GIDEON B. (1793–1867): a friend of John James Audubon. A longspur is named after him.

SNIPE: a member of a group of short-legged, long-billed shore-birds belonging to the family of *sandpipers*. Snipes are usually found in inland bogs. The North American representative of the group is the common, or Wilson's, snipe.

Common snipe

Vultures soaring

SOARING: a method of flight by which the bird glides on rising air currents without actively flapping its wings. Many birds, particularly larger ones, use this energy-saving method of flying. Examples of such birds are albatrosses and large birds of prey like the vultures. Rising air currents are encountered in many areas, for instance along cliffs, on the edge of large waves, or as thermal currents.

SOFT PARTS: a term referring to various parts of a bird, namely the covering of the bill, the iris of the eye, bare skin patches, and the bare part of the leg and foot.

SONG: vocalization, usually associated with reproductive behavior. The song consists of one or more sounds which are more or less consistently repeated in a specific pattern.

Although the best songsters are to be found among *passerines* (songbirds), many *nonpasserines* have typical songs. Thus, many shorebirds have characteristic and sometimes quite elaborate songs. In other birds *instrumental song* replaces the vocal song. An example is the drumming of woodpeckers.

The song is produced in the *syrinx,* a part of the *respiratory system* unique to birds. In many species the male alone sings, but in others the female will also sing, although usually less vigorously. A special type of song is the so-called "duetting," in which male and female sing simultaneously. In some tropical species the male and female sing in an alternating fashion so precisely timed that the singing sounds like one, not two, birds vocalizing. This is called antiphonal singing.

The complexity of the song varies tremendously from species to species. It may be simple, as in the house sparrow, or highly complex, as in many species of Old World warblers or in thrushes. In general the most complex songs are found among birds in which the sexes are quite similar and cryptic in plumage. Thus, the celebrated nightingale is a plain brown bird with the male and female virtually identical.

The song of individuals of the same species often varies slightly so that the individual bird can be recognized by its song alone. The same species may have different

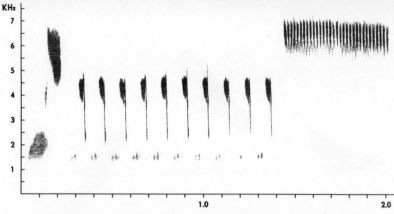

Spectrogram of the rather stereotyped song of Lark bunting

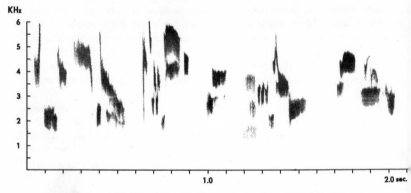

Spectrogram of the jingling song of Lapland longspur

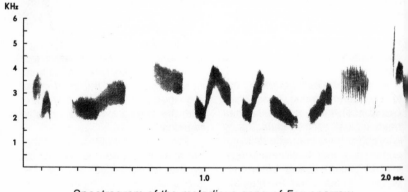

Spectrogram of the melodious song of Fox sparrow

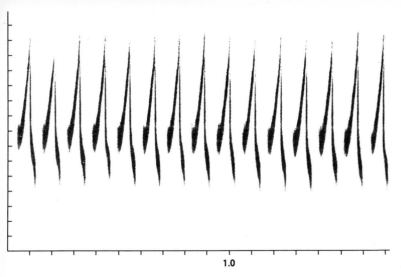

Spectrogram of the repeated figures of the song of Chipping sparrow

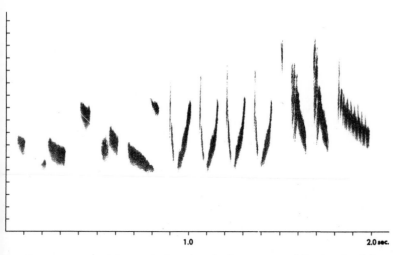

Spectrogram of the varied and melodious song of Orchard oriole

songs in different areas, so-called "dialects." The function of the song is dual: to advertise the *territory* and discourage other males from entering it, and at the same time to function as a lure for females within earshot.

Once a pair has been established the song appears to strengthen the *pair* bond. The song at this stage may be completely different from the territorial song. Similar or different, both songs are termed primary songs.

Young birds may start singing before they are ready to breed. Their song, the subsong or secondary song, is usually much simpler and given with less vigor than the primary song.

Songs are given most frequently in the early period of the breeding cycle when males are establishing their territories and attracting mates. At this time the bird may be singing almost continually. The red-eyed vireo of North America has been counted to give more than 20,000 songs in less than ten hours.

In most areas the song activity is at its peak in the early morning hours. The frequency then drops during the day, but increased song activity can often be observed near sunset. Some birds, like the nightingale, may sing throughout most of the night. Song activity is often suppressed by rain and overcast skies.

The song is in part inherited, in part learned. In most species a simple framework of the song is inherited but the full song has to be learned by listening to other birds of the same kind. Some species, particularly parrots and mynahs, are especially capable of mimicking other sounds (see *mimicry*).

Bird songs can be recorded on tape. Special equipment is usually necessary to get good recordings. The song can then be transcribed to a so-called spectrogram (or sonagram), an example of which is shown. The spectrogram, which gives information as to pitch (the height of the graph), the loudness of the note (thickness of the line), as well as the speed and number of notes, allows close analysis of bird songs. However, spectrograms are difficult to interpret, requiring quite extensive experience to be practically useful in identification of birds.

SONGBIRD: a species belonging to the order *Passeriformes*.

SPARROW: a term used for many species of the family of *New World seed-eaters* (Fringillidae), which also contains *buntings* and *cardinals*, as well as for some members of the family of *weaver finches*. Sparrows are small, rather dull-colored brown or gray birds, usually without striking patterns.

The sparrows of the New World seed-eater family are found in many different habitats ranging from desert to forest in the New World. Outside the breeding season most are social in their habits. They live mainly on seeds which they find on the ground. Some are quite accomplished songsters. Some of the more widespread and well-known North American species are the song sparrow, chipping sparrow, vesper sparrow, white-crowned sparrow, and fox sparrow.

The sparrows belonging to the family of weaver finches occur naturally only in the Old World, Africa harboring the largest number of species. Many are social in nesting habits and build large bulky nests in trees. Others are hole-nesters. The house sparrow, which belongs to this group, has been successfully introduced to many parts of the world outside its natural range. Its close association with man has made it one of the most widespread and numerous of all birds.

Song sparrow

Fox sparrow

White-crowned sparrow

Lapland longspur

Chipping sparrow

SPECIES: a term used in *taxonomy* to denote a population of birds which possess common characteristics distinguishing them from other populations and which are reproductively isolated. If two different species cross-breed, the offspring, *hybrids*, are often sterile.

SPECULUM: a brightly colored area of the wing of some waterfowl. The color of the speculum is often helpful in identification. It is displayed during courtship.

SPHENISCIFORMES: an order containing the single family of the *penguins*.

Speculum of mallard

Roseate spoonbill

Eurasian spoonbill

are social in habits. The North American representative is the roseate spoonbill found in the extreme south only.

SQUAB: a large nestling of a pigeon.

STARLING: a member of the family Sturnidae. The 107 species of starlings are indigenous to the Old World and Australia, but several species have been successfully introduced in the New World. Starlings are medium-sized passerines with strong pointed bills. Most are black or brown in color, often with white markings. Starlings inhabit a large variety of habitats and often associate themselves with man. Outside the breeding season they are social in their habits, often occurring in enor-

SPOONBILL: a member of the subfamily Plataleinae which together with *ibises* forms the family Plataleidae. The six species of spoonbills are found in tropical and subtropical wetlands throughout the world. They are large, mainly white or pink, long-legged birds with a highly characteristic long spatule-shaped bill. Spoonbills live on small aquatic animals caught as the wide bill is swept sideways on the surface of the water. They

Rose-colored starling

Starling

mous flocks. Most are hole-nesters. Many are good songsters and some, like the mynahs, are excellent mimics.

STELLER, GEORG WILHELM (1709–1746): a German-born naturalist who in Russian service explored the Bering Sea area. An eider and a jay are named after him.

STILT: a term used for some members of the family of *avocets*.

STONE CURLEW: a member of the family Burhinidae, sometimes called thick-knees. The nine species of stone curlews inhabit open country on all continents with the exception of North America and Antarctica. Stone curlews are medium-sized shorebirds with long legs and rather short, stout bills. They are streaked brown. Stone curlews live on small animals caught on the ground. They are shy birds, difficult to observe.

Stone curlew

199

White stork

Wood stork

Maribou stork

Jabiru stork

STORK: a member of the family Ciconiidae. The seventeen species of stork inhabit marshy open country on all continents except Antarctica. They are very large, long-legged and long-necked birds with long pointed bills. Most are black and/or white with bold patterns. Their wings are long and broad and many are habitual soarers. Some storks are social in habits. Storks live on animal food caught on land or in marshes. Some, like the maribu stork of Africa, are carrion eaters. These latter have almost naked heads and necks. The only North American representative of the family is the wood stork, sometimes called wood ibis, which inhabits swamps in the south.

200

STORM PETREL: a member of the family Oceanitidae. The twenty species of storm petrels are pelagic birds found throughout the world. They are small birds related to *albatrosses* and *shearwaters*. Most are black and/or white. They are excellent flyers that fly low above the ocean waves in an almost butterfly-like fashion. Several have forked tails. Storm petrels nest colonially in holes in the ground, usually on offshore islands. They are mostly nocturnal in habits on the breeding grounds. Storm petrels live on marine animals. In North America the ashy, forktailed, and Leach's petrel are found breeding. Wilson's petrel, one of the most numerous of all birds, nests on islands in the Southern Hemisphere and visits northern waters during the southern winter (the northern summer).

Cape pigeon

Leach's petrel

Wilson's petrel

STRIGIFORMES: an order containing the families of *barn owls* and *owls*.

STRUTHIONIFORMES: an order containing the single family of *ostriches*.

STRUTTING GROUND: the display ground used by the sage grouse of North America where males gather to display for the females.

SUBSONG: the *song* given by some birds before the full or primary song of the breeding season. The subsong is usually lower and quieter than the full song.

SUBSPECIES: a term used in taxonomy to denote the local population of birds with characters differing from other populations of the species. Subspecies is used synonymously with race.

Many species are comprised of two or more subspecies which replace each other geographically. In areas where subspecies meet, interbreeding occurs, resulting in fully fertile offspring containing characteristics of both parents.

SUGAR BIRD: a term used for some species of *honey-eaters*.

SUNBIRD: a member of the family Nectariniidae. The 116 species of sunbirds are found in woodlands and semiopen country in Africa, Asia, and Australia. Sunbirds are small passerines with long, slender, decurved bills and brightly metallic-colored plumages. The females are less brightly colored than the males. In several species the male has elongated tail feathers. Sunbirds feed on nectar, often obtained while the bird hovers in front of the flower like a humming-

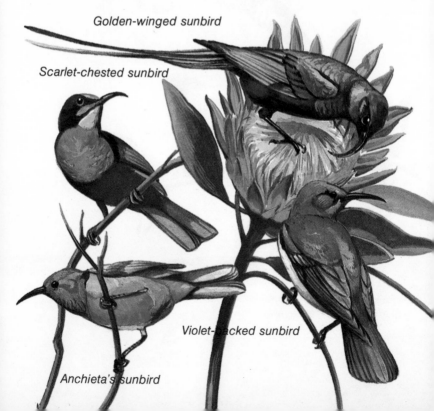

Golden-winged sunbird

Scarlet-chested sunbird

Violet-backed sunbird

Anchieta's sunbird

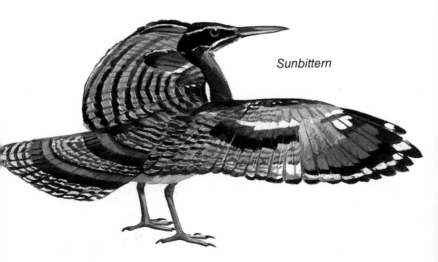

Sunbittern

bird. They also eat some insects. Sunbirds build elaborate pendant covered nests.

SUNBITTERN: the single member of the family Eurypygidae. The sunbittern is found along streams and ponds of the forests of Central and South America. It is a rather large, long-necked, broad-tailed bird with a straight pointed bill. The plumage is mottled brownish with bold orange patterns on the wings displayed only when the wing is unfolded. Sunbitterns are solitary and shy in habits.

SUPERCILIARY: a marking above the eye, usually a stripe.

SWAINSON, WILLIAM (1789–1855): English naturalist who worked in Europe, the Americas and New Zealand. A hawk, a thrush and a warbler are named after him.

SWALLOW: a member of the family Hirundinidae. The seventy-nine species of swallows inhabit open and semiopen country throughout the world excepting New Zealand and Antarctica. Swallows are small passerines with long pointed wings and forked tails. The legs are very short and the bill is weak, but with a wide gape. The plumage is usually black, brown or white, often

Cliff swallow in nest

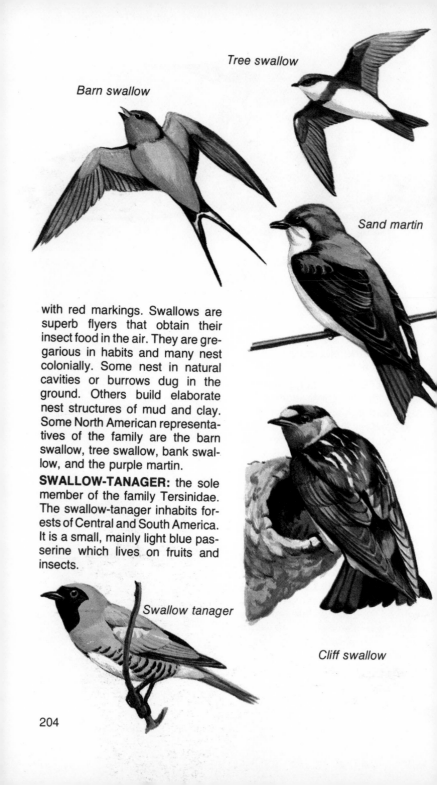

Tree swallow

Barn swallow

Sand martin

with red markings. Swallows are superb flyers that obtain their insect food in the air. They are gregarious in habits and many nest colonially. Some nest in natural cavities or burrows dug in the ground. Others build elaborate nest structures of mud and clay. Some North American representatives of the family are the barn swallow, tree swallow, bank swallow, and the purple martin.

SWALLOW-TANAGER: the sole member of the family Tersinidae. The swallow-tanager inhabits forests of Central and South America. It is a small, mainly light blue passerine which lives on fruits and insects.

Swallow tanager

Cliff swallow

SWAN: a member of the subfamily Cygninae which is part of the family Anatidae (*ducks, geese* and swans). The six species of swans are very large, long-necked white or black waterfowl found in most parts of the world. Outside the breeding season swans are gregarious. The mute swan of Eurasia and the black swan of Australia have been introduced as ornamental birds in many parts of the world. The two species indigenous to North America are the whistling swan and the once almost extinct trumpeter swan, the heaviest of flying birds.

Trumpeter swan

Black-necked swan

Mute swan

White-throated swift

Chimney swift

SWIFT: a member of the family Apodidae. The sixty-six species of swifts are found in open and semi-open country throughout the world with the exception of New Zealand and Antarctica. Swifts are small, very long-winged birds having a small bill with a wide gape used for catching insects in the air. Most are rather dull-colored black or brown. Swifts are excellent flyers and are even able to copulate and sleep on the wing. Most are colonial in habits. The nest is held together by saliva and some are *edible nests*. The most common North American species is the chimney swift.

SYRINX: the vocal organ unique to birds. The syrinx is part of the *respiratory system* and is the place where the *song* is produced. It is situated at the lower end of the trachea where this divides into the bronchi. The syrinx varies enormously in size and shape from species to species. It is supplied with muscles by the help of which its shape can be changed, varying the sound produced by the air flowing through it.

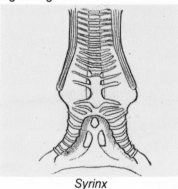

Syrinx

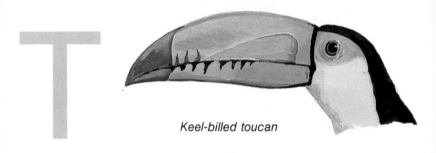

Keel-billed toucan

TAIL: the feathers attached to the rump of a bird.

The main tail feathers are called rectrices. Most birds have twelve rectrices, but the number may vary from six to thirty-two. The shape of the tail varies enormously from species to species. In some, like kiwis, it is virtually nonexistent, while in others, like the pheasants, it is very large. The shape varies and may be square, rounded, wedgelike, or forked. In general the tail is important as a balancing instrument, particularly in flight. Soaring birds usually have wide tails, whereas more agile flyers,

Birds' tails take many shapes as shown here and on the following page.

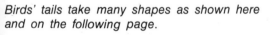

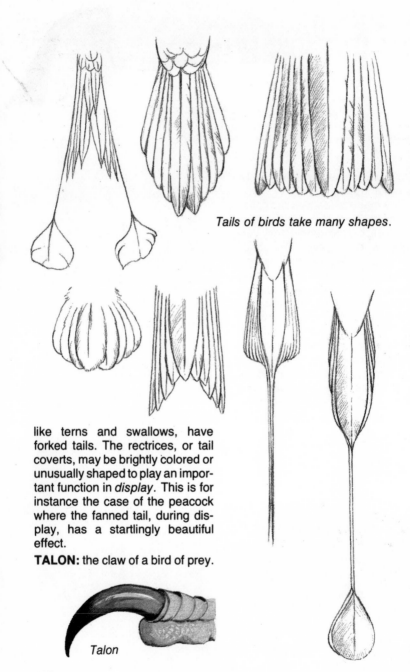

Tails of birds take many shapes.

like terns and swallows, have forked tails. The rectrices, or tail coverts, may be brightly colored or unusually shaped to play an important function in *display*. This is for instance the case of the peacock where the fanned tail, during display, has a startlingly beautiful effect.

TALON: the claw of a bird of prey.

Talon

208

TANAGER: a member of the family Thraupidae. The 223 species of tanagers are found in woods and shrublands throughout most of the New World. They are small to medium-sized passerines, which in general are brightly colored and boldly patterned in black, blue, red and yellow. Tanagers are solitary in habits. Some build elaborate domed nests. Tanagers are good songsters. The North American representatives of this colorful family are the scarlet, summer, hepatic and western tanagers.

Hooded tanager

Blue-winged mountain tanager

Golden-crowned tanager

Western tanager

Grey gallito

TAPACULO: a member of the family Rhinocryptidae. The twenty-seven species of tapaculos inhabit mountainous regions of Central and South America. They are small- to medium-sized passerines with short wings and tail. The legs are relatively long. The plumage is mainly dull brown or black. Tapaculos are ground-dwelling birds with a habit of holding their tail erect in the fashion of wrens. Most are solitary in habits.

TARSUS: the part of the avian leg from the ankle to the toes. In most birds the tarsus is covered with scales, but in some, like the golden eagle and some owls, it is covered with feathers.

TAXIDERMY: the art of stuffing and mounting animal skins.

TAXONOMY: the science of *classification*.

Taxonomy is concerned with a grouping of animals and plants. Birds belong to the kingdom of animals (Animalia). Within the kingdom they belong to the phylum of backboned animals (Chordata) and within that phylum to the class of birds (Aves).

Classification accepted today is based on phylogeny, the evolutionary history of a species or group of species. Species which are believed to have common ancestors are grouped together in a genus. The *binominal system*, by which the first part of the scientific name is that of the genus, the second, that of the species, reflects this grouping. Genera related to each other form a family, and closely related families an order. All the orders of birds then form the class of birds. To give an example of how one species fits into this classification, that of the house sparrow (*Passer domesticus*) is given below:

Species: *domesticus* (house)
Genus: *Passer* (sparrow)
Family: Ploceidae (weaver finches)
Order: Passeriformes (perching birds)
Class: Aves (birds)

Some authorities subdivide some of the larger groupings further into subclasses and superorders.

The taxonomist depends in his study on several disciplines to help him in classification. Anatomy, especially of the bony structures, is important, but biochemical, physiological and behavioral aspects are also taken into consideration. As methods of investigating these aspects become more sophisticated, modification of the current classification is made.

When a species is divided into two or more subspecies these are identified by a third name added to the specific name.

Sooty tern

Common tern

TERN: a member of the subfamily Sterninae which together with *gulls* forms the family Laridae. The thirty-nine species of terns are found throughout the world. They are medium-sized to large, usually white-and-black birds with short legs and pointed bills. Most terns live on fish or other aquatic animals caught by diving headlong into the water, or by gracefully picking the prey off the surface. Terns mainly inhabit seashores, but some may be found along inland waters. They are colonial in nesting habits. The more common North American representatives of the subfamily are the common, arctic, least, Forster's and Caspian terns.

TERRITORY: an area defended by a bird against members of its own species. Two kinds of territories are recognized, the breeding territory and the nonbreeding territory.

Most birds have breeding territories which serve several functions. The territory may be the mating and nesting area which also supplies food for adults and young. Such is, for instance, the territory of chaffinches, robins and most other passerines. The territory may be used for mating and nesting alone. Such territories are found among colonially nesting species, as well as others. The territory may finally be used for mating alone, as found among species with *lek* display.

The nonbreeding territories are usually feeding grounds and may be permanent in nature, the birds using the same area for a breeding territory also, or it may be transient, as in migratory species. Another type of territory is the roosting territory used at night. Different species vary in their degree of territorialism which is variable through the year and may be influenced by such factors as weather and availability of food and cover. *Display* and *song* play important roles in the defense of the territory.

THICK-KNEE: a term used synonymously with *stone curlew*.

THRUSH: a member of the family Turdidae. The 303 species of thrushes are found throughout the world with the exception of New Zealand and Antarctica. They are small- to medium-sized passerines with slim, straight bills and moderately strong legs. Thrushes vary greatly in plumage colors and many are spotted. They may be found in habitats varying from deserts to forests, but most are

Robin

La Selle thrush

Wood thrush

found in scrubland or woods. Many are excellent songsters. Outside the nesting season many are social in habits. Some of the more widespread North American representatives of this attractive family are the American robin, hermit thrush, Swainson's thrush, and the veery. The European robin also belongs to this family, as do the many species of wheatears.

TINAMIFORMES: the order containing the single family of the *tinamous*.

TINAMOU: a member of the family Tinamidae. The forty species of tinamous are found only in Central and South America where they inhabit various habitats from open grasslands to forests. Tinamous are medium-sized, somewhat quail-like, brown, ground-dwelling birds. They live mainly on seeds and berries. Parental care is done by the male alone. Tinamous are solitary in habits.

TITMOUSE: a member of the family Paridae. The sixty-four species of titmice are found in wooded

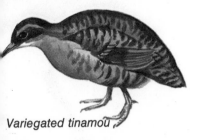

Variegated tinamou

country in North America, Eurasia and Africa. Titmice are small, short-billed, often colorful passerines. They are very active but often very tame birds. Outside the breeding season many are social in habits.

Blue tit

Titmice live on seeds and insects. Most nest in tree cavities. Several species are easily attracted to bird feeders and bird houses. In North America the several species are called chickadees, of which the black-capped chickadee is the most widespread. Other representatives are the tufted titmouse and the bushtit.

TODY: a member of the family Todidae. The five species of todies are limited in distribution to the Caribbean Islands where they are found in scrubland and woods. They are small, long-billed birds with green upper parts and red throats. Todies live on insects caught in flycatcher fashion.

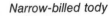

Narrow-billed tody

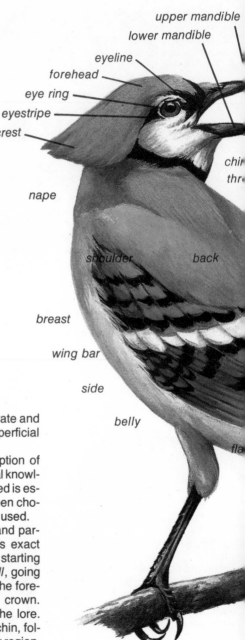

upper mandible

lower mandible

eyeline

forehead

eye ring

eyestripe

crest

nape

shoulder   back

breast

wing bar

side

belly

chin

throat

TOPOGRAPHY: the accurate and detailed description of superficial features of a bird.

For the accurate description of a bird a certain fundamental knowledge of the terminology used is essential. The bluejay has been chosen to illustrate the terms used.

In describing the head and particular facial color patterns exact description is necessary: starting at the upper base of the *bill*, going backward, the first part is the forehead, followed by the crown. Going toward the eye is the lore. Underneath the bill is the chin, followed by the throat or gular region. If a line defines the sides of the

214

chin and throat, this line is called a whisker. Surrounding the eye may be an eye-ring and above it a superciliary stripe. If there is a line through the eye, it is called an eyeline. Behind the eye are the ear coverts, or ear patches. As the head merges into the neck, the nape is found posteriorly blending into the hind neck, followed by the back which, right above the tail, becomes the rump. On either side of the body are the sides which posteriorly become the flanks. Anteriorly the breast blends into the belly. The *wing* may have wing bars, shoulder patches, or a *speculum*. At the root of the wing are the scapulars and the axillary feathers above and below respectively. The tail has upper and lower tail coverts.

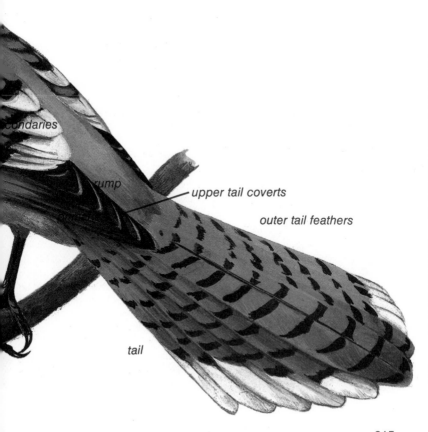

condaries

rump

upper tail coverts

outer tail feathers

tail

Lesser Wagler's toucan

Spot-billed toucanet

Laminated hill toucan

TORPIDITY: a state of lowered body temperature and metabolic state approaching *hibernation*. Members of the families of swifts, nighthawks and hummingbirds can become torpid when resting, thus preserving energy.

TOUCAN: a member of the family Ramphastidae. The thirty-seven species of toucans are found in rain forests of Central and South America. Toucans are medium-sized to large birds with enormously enlarged hollow bills. They are mainly black with bold patterns of yellow and red. Toucans live on fruits. They are often met with in small flocks. They nest in tree cavities.

TOURACO: a member of the family Musophagidae. The eighteen species of touracos are found in the jungles of Africa. Touracos are rather large, long-tailed and long-necked birds. The color varies from blue to gray with red markings. Touracos live on fruits and insects found in the canopy.

TOWNSEND, JOHN KIRK (1809–1851): American naturalist after whom a warbler and a solitaire are named.

TRAILL, THOMAS STEWART (1781–1862): Scottish physician and naturalist after whom a flycatcher is named.

TREECREEPER: a member of the family Climacteridae, also known as Australian treecreepers to distinguish them from *creepers*. The six species of Australian treecreepers are found in the woods of Australia and New Guinea. They are small, rather plain-colored tree-climbing passerines which live on insects.

Schalow's touraco

Ross's touraco

White-browed tree-creeper

TROCHILIFORMES: the order containing the sole family of the *hummingbirds*.

Black-throated trogon

male

female

TROGON: a member of the family Trogonidae. The thirty-five species of trogons are found in tropical forests throughout the world. They are medium-sized, long-tailed, brightly colored birds which live on fruit and insects found in the canopy. They are solitary in habits. The *quetzal* belongs to this family. One species, the coppery-tailed trogon, reaches the extreme southwestern parts of the United States.

TROGONIFORMES: an order containing the sole family of *trogons*.

TROPIC-BIRD: a member of the family Phaethontidae. The three species of tropic-birds are found in the warm seas of the world. They are rather large, gull-like, black, long-tailed birds. Tropic-birds are pelagic in habits, coming to land only to breed. They live on aquatic animals caught in ternlike fashion. The red-billed and white-tailed tropic-birds may visit the coasts of North America.

Red-tailed tropicbird

TRUMPETER: a member of the family Psophidae. The three species of trumpeters are found in the rain forests of northern South America. They are rather large, long-legged, blackish ground-dwelling birds. Trumpeters live on fruits and insects. They have earned their name from the trumpeting call of the male.

TUBENOSE: a term used for a member of the order *Procellariiformes*.

TURKEY: a member of the family Meleagrididae. The two species of turkeys are found in woodlands of North and Central America. Turkeys are very large fowl-like birds. The plumage is generally colored black and brown. The tail is long and fan-shaped. The neck and head are bare. Turkeys have been successfully domesticated since

White-winged trumpeter

the time of Columbus. In North America the turkey has become extinct in many areas but attempts to reintroduce the species have met with success in many cases, and the species is extending its range.

Turkey

Scissor-tailed flycatcher

Spooted tody flycatcher

Vermillion flycatcher

Eastern wood pewee

Western kingbird

TURNSTONE: a term used for several members of the family of *sandpipers*.

TYRANT FLYCATCHER: a member of the family Tyrannidae. The 367 species of tyrant flycatchers are found in the Americas only, where they inhabit forests as well as semiopen country. They are small to medium-sized passerines, most of which are rather plainly colored green, yellow, or gray. Notable exceptions are such brightly colored species as the vermilion flycatcher. Tyrant flycatchers live on insects caught in the air. Many are pugnacious birds. They are solitary in habits. In North America some of the more common and widespread representatives of this large family are the eastern and western kingbirds, the great-crested and ash-throated flycatchers, Hammond's, western and Traill's flycatchers, the eastern and western phoebe, and the eastern and western wood pewee.

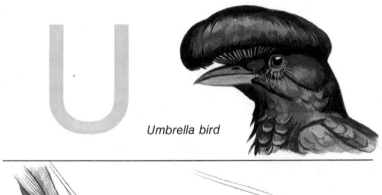

Umbrella bird

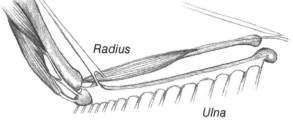

Radius

Ulna

ULNA: a bone of the *wing* which together with the radius forms the forearm, to which the *secondary* feathers are attached.

UMBRELLA BIRD: a term used for several members of the family of *cotingas*, which are found in South America. They are named from the umbrella-like crest with which they are adorned.

UNDER PARTS: the lower surface of a bird from the chin to the tip of the tail.

UNDULATING: a term used to denote the waving flight of certain birds, for instance woodpeckers.

UPPER PARTS: the upper surface of a bird from the forehead to the tip of the tail.

URINARY SYSTEM: part of the *excretory system*, consisting of the two kidneys and the urinary tracts.

UROPYGIAL GLAND: the *oil gland*.

Undulation flight of red-bellied woodpecker

Philadelphia vireo

VAGRANT: a term used to denote a bird which has wandered outside its normal breeding, wintering, and migratory range.

VANE: the flat part of a *feather* consisting of the *barbs*, extending on each side of the *rachis*.

VANGA SHRIKE: a member of the family Vangidae. The thirteen species of vanga shrikes inhabit wooded country on the island of Madagascar. Vanga shrikes are small- to medium-sized passerines with heavy bills. They are mainly black, blue and white in color. Vanga shrikes live on small animals and insects caught among the branches and foliage. They are social in habits.

VASCULAR SYSTEM: the organs involved in the circulation of blood and lymph. The central part of the vascular system is the heart, a muscular pump situated in the thoracic cavity. The heart consists of four chambers, as in mammals—two atriae or auricles and two ventricles. The blood entering

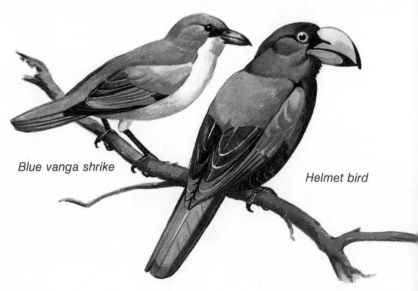

Blue vanga shrike

Helmet bird

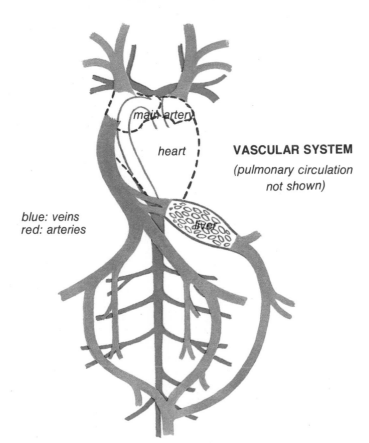

main artery

heart

blue: veins
red: arteries

liver

VASCULAR SYSTEM

*(pulmonary circulation
not shown)*

the right atrium is shunted into the right ventricle when the heart relaxes (diastole) from where, during the heart's contraction (systole), it is pumped into the arteries supplying the lungs. In the lungs the blood gives off carbon dioxide and absorbs oxygen. From the lungs the oxygenated blood enters the left atrium from where it flows into the left ventricle during diastole. From the left ventricle it is pumped into the aorta during systole. Through arteries, arterioles and capillaries the blood reaches the venous system which returns the blood to the right atrium. During its passage through the capillaries the blood gives off oxygen as well as nutrients to the tissues. The nutrients are absorbed directly into the bloodstream as well as indirectly through the lymphatic system from the *alimentary canal*. In birds the great metabolic rate associated with the demands of flight has caused the development of an extremely efficient vascular system, and the heart is relatively large. The heartbeats vary in rate from 60 per minute (the same as humans) in the ostrich to more than 1,000 per minute in hummingbirds.

VAUX, WILLIAM SAMSON (1811–1882): American naturalist and archeologist after whom a swift is named.

VENTRAL: a term used to denote the underside of the body of the bird.

VERRAUX, JULES PIERRE (1807–1873): French naturalist who together with his brothers traveled widely in Africa, Asia and Australia where he collected vast numbers of birds. Among other animals an African eagle is named after him.

VIREO: a member of the family Vireonidae. The thirty-seven species of vireos are found in wooded country in North, Central and South America. Vireos are small, plain-colored passerines. They are rather sluggish in behavior. Most live on insects found among the foliage but have rather strong bills. Many are accomplished singers. Vireos are solitary in habits. Among the more wide-spread representatives of the family in North America are the solitary, the red-eyed, and the warbling vireos.

Black vulture

VISITOR: a term used to denote a bird which is present in certain areas for only a part of the year.

VULTURE: a term used for fourteen species of the family of *hawks*, also called Old World vultures to distinguish them from the members of the family of *New World vultures*. Vultures are large, broad-winged, scavenging birds of prey found in southern Eurasia and Africa. They inhabit mainly open country. Vultures are generally brown or black in color. They often congregate around carcasses and near garbage dumps.

Yellow-throated vireo

Grey vireo

Yellow-shafted flicker

WADER: a term used synonymously with *shorebird*.

WAGTAIL: a term used for some members of the family Motacillidae, which also includes the *pipit*. Wagtails are small, long-tailed, soft-billed passerines which are found throughout the Old World with the exception of Australia. Two species, the white and the yellow wagtail, have crossed the Bering Strait to Alaska. Wagtails are ground-dwelling black, white, or yellow birds of open country. They have earned their name from their habit of wagging their tail incessantly up and down.

WARBLER: a small, soft-billed songbird, generally belonging to the families of *Old World warblers* or *wood-warblers*.

WATERFOWL: a term used to denote both the order Anseriformes and the family Anatidae comprised of *ducks, geese* and *swans*.

Wattled crow

Huia

Pied wagtail

WATTLEBIRD: a member of the family Callaeidae. The two species of wattlebirds inhabit the woods of New Zealand. Wattlebirds are medium-sized passerines, black, blue and brown in color, with brightly colored wattles at the gape. One of the species, the huia, has recently become extinct.

225

Red-faced waxbill *Yellow-bellied waxbill*

WAXBILL: a member of the family Estrildidae. The 107 species of waxbills are found in open or semi-open country in Africa, Asia, and Australia. Waxbills are small, brightly colored finchlike birds with strong conical bills. They are highly social in habits and build large domed nests. Several species are favored cage birds.

WAXWING: a member of the family Bombycillidae. The three species of waxwings are found in the forests of the northern part of the Northern Hemisphere. Waxwings are medium-sized, crested passerines. They are social in habits outside the breeding season. Waxwings often perform *irruptions* of areas outside their normal range. They live mainly on berries. The North American representatives are the cedar and the bohemian waxwings.

Cedar waxwing

WEAVER FINCH: a member of the family Ploceidae. The 156 species of weaver finches are indigenous to Eurasia and Africa, but members of the family, particularly the house sparrow, have been successfully introduced to most parts of the world. Weaver finches are small seed-eating passerines. They vary greatly in color and some have very long tails. Weaver finches are very social in habits. Some species build enormous communal nests. Their intricate nest building has earned the group its name. Some are *parasitic*. Some weaver finches occur in enormous flocks and can cause severe damage to crops, as for instance the *quelea*.

WEIGHT: Among birds, weight varies from the 1/10 of an ounce of the bee hummingbird to the 300 pounds of the ostrich. The heaviest flying bird is the trumpeter swan which may weigh more than 35 pounds. Individual birds vary in weight with age (see *growth*) as well as with season. Most migratory species attain their greatest weight just prior to *migration* as fat is stored for the journey.

WHISTLER: a member of the family Pachycephalidae, also called shrike thrush. The forty-two species of whistlers inhabit Australia and the neighboring islands. Whistlers are small passerines with heavy bills. They are rather dull-colored green, yellow, brown,

Social weaver

Golden whistler

and gray. Whistlers prefer semi-open country where they hunt insects in the branches of trees and scrubs. They are solitary in habits.

WHITE-EYE: a member of the family Zosteropidae. The ninety species of white-eyes inhabit woods and shrublands of Africa, Asia, and Australia. They are very small, mainly green and yellow warblerlike birds which live mainly on insects caught in the foliage. Their white eye-ring has earned the family its name. White-eyes are often met with in flocks. Several are good singers.

Cinnamon white-eye

WIED, PRINCE OF, MAXIMILLIAN ALEXANDER PHILLIP (1782–1867): German prince and naturalist who travelled widely in North and South America. A fly-catcher is named after him.

WILDFOWL: a term used synonymously with *game bird,* but sometimes restricted to *waterfowl.*

An example of A. Wilsons art

WILSON, ALEXANDER (1766–1813): Scottish-born American

228

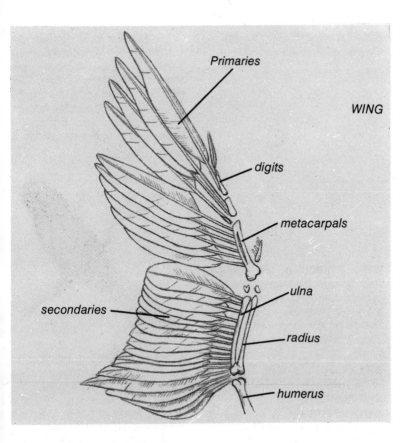

Primaries

digits

metacarpals

secondaries

ulna

radius

humerus

naturalist and artist who produced a nine-volume illustrated treatise on the birds of eastern North America. A petrel, plover, phalarope and warbler are named after him.

WING: the forelimb of a bird, which in all but the *flightless bird* has been modified for flight. The wings of flying birds vary much in both shape and size. Thus, the wings of soaring birds are broad and rounded, whereas in hummingbirds for instance they are pointed and narrow. The length of the wing varies from that of the virtually wingless kiwi to the more than 4½ feet of the wing of the wandering albatross. Feathers of the wing, particularly *primaries* and *secondaries*, give it its size. They attach to the forelimb consisting of the humerus, the forearm (the ulnar and radial bones), and the hand and fingers, of which usually only three are preserved. The wing is attached to the body via the shoulder which is a joint connecting the humerus to the shoulder girdle. The main muscle involved in the movement of the wing is the pectoral muscle which attaches to the keel of the breastbone.

Wing formulae of Blyth's reed warbler and marsh warbler

WING FORMULA: the relationship between the length of various primary feathers. Wing formulas are of importance in the identification of several *Old World warblers* which are otherwise very similar.

WOODCOCK: a term used for some members of the family of *sandpipers*.

WOODCREEPER: a member of the family Dendrocolaptidae. The forty-eight species of woodcreepers are limited in distribution

Red-billed woodcreeper

to the woodlands of Central and South America. Woodcreepers are small- to medium-sized passerines of dull brown colors. They find their insect food by climbing tree trunks in woodpecker fashion. Woodcreepers are solitary in habits and nest in tree cavities.

Cape red-billed hoopoe

WOODHOOPOE: a member of the family Phoeniculidae. The six species of woodhoopoes are limited in distribution to the wooded areas of Africa. They are medium-sized, long-tailed, long-billed birds with black metallic plumage. Woodhoopoes live mainly on insects caught among the foliage, but may eat fruits. They are solitary in habits.

WOODPECKER: a member of the family Picidae. The 208 species of woodpeckers are found throughout the world excepting Australia and Antarctica. They are dependent on the presence of trees for survival. Woodpeckers are small- to medium-sized, often boldly patterned birds. They are highly specialized in excavating and extracting insects from tree trunks. They have chisel-shaped bills with which they are able to demolish

Yellow-naped
woodpecker

Red-headed
woodpecker

Yellow-bellied
sapsucker

Downy
woodpecker

even the hardest of woods. The tail is short and stiff and used as a prop as the woodpecker climbs the tree trunk in search for food. Woodpeckers nest in holes of tree trunks they excavate with their bill. Some of the more common North American species are the yellow-shafted and red-shafted flickers, yellow-bellied sapsuckers, and the hairy and downy woodpeckers.

WOOD-SWALLOW: a member of the family Artamidae. The ten species of wood-swallows inhabit semiopen country of Australia and southern Asia. They are medium-sized passerines of rather plain brown, black and gray colors. Wood-swallows are excellent flyers which catch insects in the air. They are social in habits.

Magnolia warbler

Parula warbler

WOOD-WARBLER: a member of the family Parulidae. The 118 species of wood-warblers are limited in distribution to wooded country of the Americas. Wood-warblers live on insects found in the foliage. They are small, soft-billed, often boldly colored passerines which find their homes in trees and bushes. Wood-warblers are solitary in habits. In North America more than fifty species are found nesting. Some of the more common and widespread are the black and white, orange-crowned, parula, yellow, magnolia, myrtle, black-throated green, blackpol, pine, prairie, and palm warblers, as well as the oven-bird, northern water-thrush, yellow-throat, and American redstart.

WREN: a member of the family Troglodytidae. The fifty-nine species of wrens are found throughout the world except Australia, southern Africa and Antarctica. Wrens are small passerines with brown, barred plumage. Most have short

Winter wren

Bewick's wren

tails held vertically. Wrens are active birds, mainly found in areas with dense cover. They live on insects. They are solitary in their habits. The more common North American representatives of the family are the house, Bewick's, Carolina, and long-billed marsh wrens.

WREN-TIT: the single member of the family Chamaeidae. The wren-tit is found in brushlands of western North America. It is a small, long-tailed brown passerine.

WREN-WARBLER: a member of the family Maluridae. The eighty-three species of wren-warblers inhabit woods and shrublands of Australia and New Zealand. Wren-warblers are small, soft-billed passerines. Many are boldly patterned in brilliant colors and have long

Wren tit

tails which are often held vertically. Wren-warblers are social in habits outside the breeding season. They build elaborate domed nests.

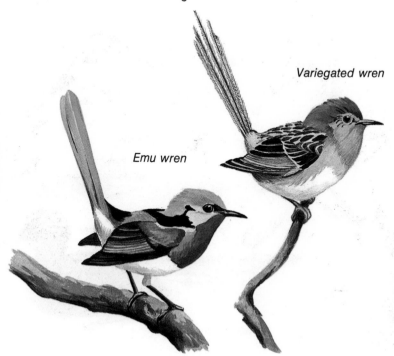

Variegated wren

Emu wren

Marsh hawk

XY

XANTHOCHROISM: a rare aberrant yellow *plumage* color.

XANTUS, JOHN (1825–1894): Hungarian naturalist after whom a murrelet is named.

YOLK: the yellow part of an *egg*.

YOUNG: a bird at the stage of life between hatching and sexual maturity (*adult*). The young bird goes through various stages: until fully grown it is called a pullus. After attaining adult size and its full feathered plumage, but before attaining sexual maturity, it is termed a juvenile or later an immature bird. The *development* and *growth* of the young bird varies tremendously from species to species.

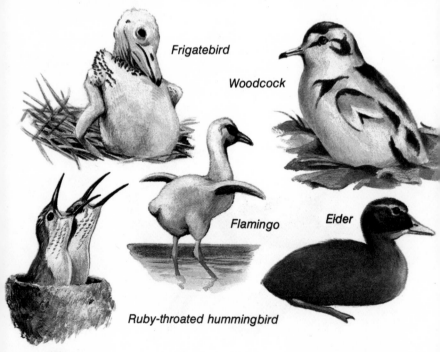

Frigatebird

Woodcock

Flamingo

Eider

Ruby-throated hummingbird

Emu

Pheasant

Blue-booted booby

Peregrine falcon

Wood thrush

Roseate tern

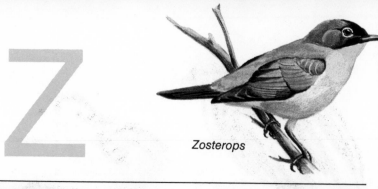

Zosterops

ZOOGEOGRAPHY: the study of the geographical *distribution* of animals. In the study of zoogeography it has been convenient to divide the world into several faunal regions within which the faunas are relatively uniform, particularly when looked upon from the viewpoint of bird families. The major faunal regions are: the Australasian region, consisting of Australia, New Guinea and New Zealand with neighboring islands; the Ethiopian region, consisting of Africa south of the Sahara Desert; the Nearctic region, consisting of North America, south to central Mexico; the Neotropical region,

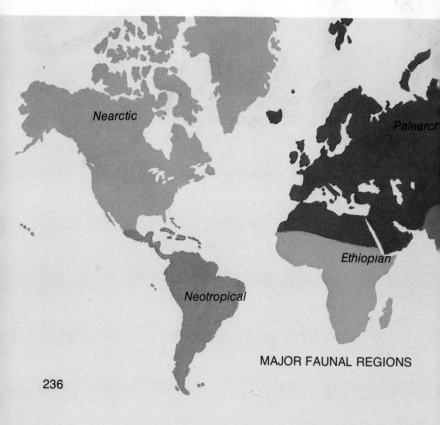

Nearctic

Palearct

Ethiopian

Neotropical

MAJOR FAUNAL REGIONS

consisting of South America and most of Central America and the Caribbean Islands; the Oriental region, consisting of southern Asia and its islands; and the Palearctic region, consisting of Europe, northern Asia and northernmost Africa. The Nearctic and the Palearctic regions together are often called the Holarctic region. Some authorities consider the islands of the Pacific Ocean a separate entity, the Oceanic region. Some also consider Madagascar and its neighboring islands a separate region from the Ethiopian, calling it the Malagay region. The Antarctic coast and islands may also be considered a separate faunal region.

ZUGUNRUHE: a term, of German origin, used to denote the restlessness of migratory and pre-migratory birds. Zugunruhe in caged, wild birds has played an important role in the investigation of *migration* and *orientation*.

ZYGODACTYL: having two toes pointed forward and one or two backward, rather than the more common three toes forward and one backward. Several birds, for instance the woodpeckers, are zygodactyl.

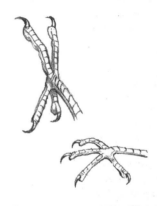

Foot of woodpecker (zygodactyl) and sparrow

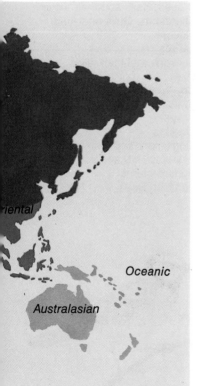

Oriental

Oceanic

Australasian

APPENDIX

Since all orders of living birds in this book are entered under their scientific names rather than their common names, we list their common names below.

Scientific Name	Commonly Used Name
Tinamiformes	Tinamous
Struthioniformes	Ostriches
Rheiformes	Rheas
Casuariiformes	Cassowaries and Emus
Apterygiformes	Kiwis
Gaviiformes	Loons
Podicipediformes	Grebes
Sphenisciformes	Penguins
Procellariiformes	Tubenoses
Pelecaniformes	Pelicans and their allies
Ardeiformes	Herons and their allies
Phoenicopgeriformes	Flamingoes
Anseriformes	Waterfowl
Falconiformes	Birds-of-Prey
Galliformes	Fowl-like Birds
Gruiformes	Cranes, Rails and their allies
Charadriiformes	Shorebirds, Gulls and Auks
Columbiformes	Pigeons
Psittaciformes	Parrots
Cuculiformes	Cuckoos and their allies
Strigiformes	Owls
Caprimulgiformes	Goatsuckers and their allies
Apodiformes	Swifts
Coliiformes	Colies
Trogoniformes	Trogons
Coraciiformes	Kingfishers and their allies
Piciformes	Woodpeckers and their allies
Trochiliformes	Hummingbirds
Passeriformes	Perching Birds

BIBLIOGRAPHY

Hundreds of books on birds are published yearly. Each country and each region has its own extensive literature and a complete listing of books on birds and their lives would fill a sizeable bookshelf. For the interested reader, however, there are listed below a number of special interest books as well as a few of the more widely-known books on bird life in general. No attempt has been made to list any of the monographs or specialized works treating families or orders, although many of these are of great importance.

Alexander, W.B.: *Birds of the Ocean*. N.Y. Putnam, 1954.

Armstrong, E.A.: *Bird Display and Behaviour*. London, Lindsay Drummond 1947.

Austin, Oliver L., Jr.: *Birds of the World*. N.Y. Golden Press 1960.

Austin, Oliver L., Jr.: *Families of Birds*. N.Y. Golden Press 1971.

Bond, J.: *Birds of the West Indies*. London, Collins 1960.

Bruun, Bertel: *Birds of Europe*. N.Y. McGraw-Hill 1971.

Davis, L.F.: *A Field Guide to the Birds of Mexico and Central America*. Austin, Univ. of Texas Press 1972.

Dementiev, G.P. and N.A. Gladkov: *Birds of the Soviet Union*. 6Vols. Moscow 1951–54.

Dorst, F.: *The Migrations of Birds*. London, Heinemann 1962.

Falla, R.A., R.B. Gibson and E.G. Turbott: *A Field Guide to the Birds of New Zealand*. London, Collins 1966.

Gilliard, E.T.: *Living Birds of the World*. N.Y., Doubleday 1958.

Greenway, F.C., Jr.: *Extinct and Vanishing Birds of the World*. N.Y., Am. Comm. Int. Wildlife Prot. 1958.

Grzimek, H.C.B. (Ed.): *Grzimek's Animal Life Encyclopedia*. Vol. 7–9., N.Y., Van Nostrand Reinhold 1972.

Mackworth-Praed, C.W. and C.H.B. Grant: *African Handbook of Birds*. *Series I-III*. London, Longmans 1953.

Peterson, R.T. & James Fisher: *The World of Birds*. N.Y. Doubleday 1963.

Peterson, Roger Tory: *A Field Guide to The Birds,* 1947; *A Field Guide to Western Birds,* 1961; *A Field Guide to the Birds of Texas and Adjacent States,* 1963. Boston, Houghton Mifflin.

Peterson, Roger Tory: *The Birds*. N.Y., Time-Life Books 1963.

Peterson, Roger Tory, Guy Mountford & P.A.D. Hollom: *A Field Guide to the Birds of Britain & Europe*. Boston, Houghton Mifflin 1966.

Pettingill, Olin S., Jr.: *Ornithology in Laboratory and Field*. Minneapolis 1970.

Rand, A.L. & E.T. Gilliard: *Handbook of New Guinea Birds*. London, Weidenfeld & Nicholson 1967.

Robbins, Chandler S., B. Bruun and H.S. Zim: *Birds of North America*. N.Y. Golden Press 1966.

de Schauensee, R.M.: *A Guide to the Birds of South America*. Wynnewood, Pa., Livingston 1970.

Slater, P.: *A Field Guide to Australian Birds*. Edinburgh, Oliver & Boyd 1971.

Sturkie, P.D.: *Avian Physiology*. Ithaca, N.Y. Comstock Publ. Ass. 1954.

Thomson, A. Landsborough (Ed.): *A New Dictionary of Birds*. N.Y., McGraw-Hill. 1964.

Thorpe, W.H.: *Bird Song*. Cambridge, Cambridge Univ. Press 1960.

Van Tyne, F. and A. Berger: *Fundamentals of Ornithology*. N.Y. John Wiley. 1959.

Vaurie, C.: *The Birds of the Palearctic Fauna*. Vol. I and II. London, Witherby 1959 & 1965.

Wetmore, Alexander: *A Classification for the Birds of the World*. Washington, D.C., Smithsonian Inst. 1960.

Williams, J.G.: *The Birds of East and Central Africa*. London, Collins 1963.

Yamashina, Y.: *Birds in Japan*. Tokyo, Tokyo News Service 1961.

SOUTH DEVON TECHNICAL
COLLEGE — LIBRARY

FOR REFERENCE ONLY

NOT TO BE TAKEN OUT
OF THE LIBRARY